PIONEERS in PROTEST

PIONEERS *in* PROTEST

By

LERONE BENNETT JR.

Johnson Publishing Company Inc.

Chicago: 1968

*Photographs on pages 182 and 232
reproduced by permission of United Press International
and European Picture Agency, respectively.*

*Copyright © 1968
Johnson Publishing Co., Inc.
SBN No. 87485-026-6*

*Library of Congress Catalog No. 68-55366
Printed in the United States of America
First edition, September, 1968
Second printing, 1969
Third printing, 1992
Fourth printing, 2000*

*For the modern pioneers
and martyrs:
Martin Luther King Jr.,
Medgar Evers, and
Malcolm X.*

CONTENTS

ROUSE
the
DAWN

---◆---

Crispus Attucks

My soul is among lions: and I lie even among them that are on fire, even the sons of men, whose teeth are spears and arrows, and their tongue a sharp sword. They have prepared a net for my steps, my soul is bowed down: they have digged a pit before me, into the midst whereof they are fallen themselves.... Awake up, my glory ... I will rouse the dawn....

FIFTY-SEVENTH PSALM

CRISPUS ATTUCKS

THE DAY dawned cold and cloudy.

There was a film of ice on the narrow cobblestone streets and a tang of tension in the Boston air.

Boston, by now, was used to tension. As the center of the burgeoning resistance movement to British colonial rule, the city was virtually controlled by fiery revolutionaries who roamed the streets smashing windows, setting fires and pelting officials with snowballs and stones. Rioting and looting were common in the city, and there was constant skirmishing between bold young men and the red-coated British troops.

The day dawning now promised to be no better and no worse than the preceding days of this riotous season. Nobody knew then that the day would end in the blood and steel of the Boston Massacre. The good burghers of the city rose early, ate well and went to the shops and offices on Washington Street. Longshoremen and laborers moved by ones and twos to the docks and factories. Indentured servants — black and white — roused themselves for another day's work in the service of their Puritan masters.

During the day, a few inches of snow fell. The sky cleared late in the afternoon; and at sunset a new moon appeared in the cloudless skies over Beacon Hill. On Beacon Hill and in Roxbury and in the ghetto of New Guinea, men — black and white — clung to the routines of a lifetime. But beneath the surface moved explosive forces that would make this day—Monday, March 5, 1770—a day to remember.

Somewhere in Boston on this day, wily old Sam Adams and the Sons of Liberty were studying revolution and setting traps and snares.

Somewhere in Boston, a black man named Crispus Attucks was moving toward a critical crossroad of history.

Somewhere in the city, Private Hugh Montgomery of the British Army was eyeing the building tension with apprehension.

Tension had been building in Boston now for eighteen months. Puritan revolutionaries were in open revolt against the government; and there was rising antagonism between well-to-do Boston Loyalists, who sided with Great Britain, and angry Patriots, who contended that taxation without representation was tyranny. When, in the winter of 1770, the colonial masses pushed their way onto the stage, the struggle reached explosive proportions. Throughout this long cold winter, the masses, who were exploited by the British and the colonists, rioted, stoned the houses of Loyalists and voiced open demands for a social as well as a political revolution. In this winter, as in the long hot summers of the Black Revolution, riots became a political weapon. Behind the scenes, talented agitators like Samuel Adams fanned the fires of discontent by organizing demonstrations, boycotts, and riots.

Black people and other low-income Bostonians, who had nothing to lose and everything to gain, were in the front ranks of this struggle. Although there were only one thousand blacks in the Boston population of twelve to fifteen thousand, patriots of color were vociferously visible in the street demonstrations and riots. Black people, for example, were among the most creative and defiant of the Stamp Act rioters. Many years later, author John Miller described one of these riots. "For a fortnight," he wrote, "the tension in Boston continued to increase, until, on the night of August 28 [1765], boys and Negroes began to build bonfires in King Street and blow the dreaded whistle that sent the Boston mob swarming out of taverns, houses, and garrets. A large crowd immediately gathered around the bonfires, bawling for 'Liberty and Property.'"

These riots led to the germinal decision to send troops to Boston. And this decision led, bullet by bullet, to the Declaration of Independence. The quartering of troops in Boston gave Sam Adams and other revolutionaries an opportunity to create a revolutionary situation. The Puritan revolutionaries made good use of this opportunity, and within a short time the position of the troops was untenable. There were provocations on both sides and a series of bloody incidents. A few months before the Boston Massacre, the Redcoats and the blacks clashed on Boston Common. A Boston newspaper commented: "In the morning nine or ten soldiers of Colonel Carr's regiment were severely whipped on the Common. To behold Britons scourged by Negro drummers was a new and very disagreeable spectacle."

Unquestionably, and yet the spectacle continued. There were repeated incidents in February. And on Friday, March 2, there was a brawl between the soldiers and the ropemakers. Ripples from this incident spread across the city, and by nightfall on Monday, March 5, Boston was boiling.

As soon as the new moon appeared over Boston Hill, the soldiers and civilians began jockeying for position. By eight o'clock, the streets were clogged with defiant men, spoiling for a fight.

Witnesses said later that a tall man, "almost a giant," dominated one segment of this wandering crowd. This man, who answered to the name Crispus Attucks, has caused traditional historians no end of trouble. In the first place, he was not a proper Bostonian. In fact, he was not even white. By singular circumstance, the hero of the Boston Massacre and the first martyr of the Revolution was a black man and a former slave.

It was Attucks who rallied the wandering crowd and focused

its fury.

It was Attucks who carried the battle to the enemy.

It was Attucks, an obscure black man, who was "the first to defy, and the first to die."

Some writers have suggested that Attucks and his colleagues were maneuvered into action by behind-the-scenes agitators who wanted to create a revolutionary point of departure. To be sure, there is some evidence to indicate that the Sons of Liberty set the stage for the disturbance. But there is no convincing evidence to indicate that Attucks acted for anyone other than himself. The record indicates, moreover, that Attucks had a deep and unquenchable love of liberty.

Six feet two, with a fierce countenance and a volatile disposition, Attucks had been born in slavery some forty-seven years before this night in Framingham, Massachusetts. In September, 1750, he struck his first blow for freedom by running away from his master. On October 2, 1750, William Brown of Framingham entered the following description of the runaway in the Boston *Gazette*: "Short, curly hair, his knees nearer together than common; had on a light colored bearskin coat, plain brown fustian jacket, or a brown wool one, new buckskin breeches, blue yarn stockings and a checked woolen shirt. Whoever shall take up said runaway, convey him to above said master, shall receive ten pounds, old tenor reward, and all necessary charges paid. And all masters of vessels, or others, are hereby cautioned against concealing or carrying off said servant on penalty of the law."

Attucks eluded his pursuers and apparently went to sea as a sailor. There is some evidence to indicate that he spent a great deal of time around the docks in lower Boston. But his movements prior to the night of the Boston Massacre are a matter of conjecture. It was said later that he was in Boston on March 5 awaiting a ship for North Carolina. However that might be, the fact remains that Attucks—bold, defiant, and adventurous

—was at center stage on the night of the first momentous act of America's birth.

This drama entered a new phase shortly after eight o'clock on the night in question when the British soldiers sallied out of Murray's Barracks and went for a stroll. This maneuver was designed apparently to prove that the soldiers were not afraid. If so, it was ill-timed and ill-considered. For the soldiers were soon embroiled in a free-for-all with the inflamed citizenry. Someone ran to the Old Brick Meeting House and rang the fire bell. Men poured out of the garrets and houses, and Boston vibrated with the sounds of incipient rebellion—the beating of drums, the ringing of bells, cries, screams, imprecations.

At about the same moment, not too far away, a sentry and a barber's apprentice exchanged insults. The sentry clubbed the youth with the butt of his musket. The youth ran screaming through the streets, embellishing the story, no doubt, as he went.

In the wake of this event, wild rumors circulated through the crowd. Some men said the sentry had stabbed the youth. Some men said they had it on good authority that the youth was already dead.

Reports of the altercation reached Crispus Attucks in Dock Square. According to one report, he exploded, saying: "The way to get rid of these soldiers is to attack the main guard. Strike at the nest!"

The Dock Square crowd, with Attucks in the forefront, surged toward King Street shouting: "Let us drive out these ribalds. They have no business here." Part of the crowd went up Royal Exchange into King Street. But the largest group followed Crispus Attucks through Boylston's Alley. Attucks was armed with a large cordwood stick. According to an eye-witness, Attucks and his men were huzzaing and whistling and carrying their sticks upright over their heads.

Before long, there was a crowd of perhaps a hundred whooping, hollering, cursing Bostonians in the little square near the Custom House. The barber's apprentice pointed to the sentry and said, "This is the ———— who hit me." The crowd shouted, "Knock him down! Kill him!"

The sentry backed up the steps of the Custom House, shoved the rammer down his musket and primed it. By this time, reinforcements—seven subalterns and Captain Thomas Preston —were pushing through the crowd.

Crispus Attucks, who was standing in the rear of the crowd, sized up the situation and seized command.

"Do not be afraid," he said. "They dare not fire."

The crowd echoed Attucks' words.

"Damn them! They dare not fire. Fire! and be damned."

Attucks and his party gave three cheers and pushed to the front of the crowd, advancing to the tips of the soldiers' bayonets. It was about nine-thirty now, and the bayonets of the beleaguered soldiers glistened in the light of the clear moon. For several seconds, Attucks and the soldiers stood face to face. Then, without warning, someone threw a stick. The stick hit Private Hugh Montgomery, who fell backwards, raised his musket and fired. Attucks, who was standing near the gutter, pitched forward, blood gushing from wounds in his chest. The crowd surged forward and other soldiers fired. When the smoke cleared, five men lay sprawled in the snow—three dead, two mortally wounded.

Like other seminal chapters in history, the events of this night pushed men across the borders of themselves. "From that moment," Daniel Webster said later, "we may date the severance of the British Empire." John Adams, America's second President, said: "On that night, the foundation of American independence was laid." He added: "Not the Battle of Lexington or Bunker Hill, not the surrender of Burgoyne or Cornwallis were more important events in American history than the Battle of King Street on the 5th of March, 1770."

Three days later, on Thursday, March 8, there was a public

funeral for Attucks and three other martyrs. All the shops in Boston closed in their honor, and all the bells of the city and neighboring towns pealed in remembrance. Contemporaries reported that "a greater number of persons assembled on this occasion, than ever before gathered on this continent for a similar purpose."

The public outcry following the funeral forced withdrawal of the British regiment to Castle Island. Seven of the soldiers were tried for murder and acquitted. Two were found guilty of manslaughter and received minimal sentences. At the trial, John Adams, the defense attorney, was critical of the Boston crowd which he called "a motley rabble of saucy boys, Negroes and mulattoes, Irish Teagues and outlandish Jack Tars." Adams said that Attucks appeared "to have undertaken to be the hero of the night; and to lead this army with banners, to form them in the first place in Dock Square, and march them up to King Street with their clubs."

Although most of the soldiers were exonerated, Attucks and his comrades were speedily transformed into exemplar myths. The date of their death was celebrated as the national holiday until the adoption of the Declaration of Independence.

One hundred and eighteen years after their death, a monument was erected to the martyrs on Boston Common. John Boyle O'Reilly wrote a special poem for the occasion.

And honor to Crispus Attucks, who was leader and voice that day:
The first to defy, and the first to die, with Maverick, Carr, and
    Gray.
Call it riot or revolution, or mob or crowd as you may,
Such deaths have been seeds of nations, such lives shall be honored
    for ay . . .

THE STARGAZER

Benjamin Banneker

*Look back, I entreat
you . . .*

BENJAMIN BANNEKER

BENJAMIN BANNEKER

EVERY NIGHT, as soon as the moon appeared over the hills on the Patapsco River, the black farmer stole from his cabin with a cloak and pencil and paper. Spreading the cloak on the ground, oblivious of the startled gaze of prying neighbors, the man took up his favorite position: flat on his back, hands under his head, eyes fixed on the fireflies of stars and suns hundreds of light years away. Until dawn, until the stars melted away in light, the stargazer maintained his vigil. Then, brushing himself off, he retreated, absentmindedly, into the cabin where neighbors, in search of salt or information, found him asleep at midday.

The good dull farmers of Ellicott's Lower Mills (now Ellicott City), near Baltimore, were shocked. Good farmers didn't act that way. A farmer, it was said, should be up and doing in the morning and early to bed at night.

What kind of behavior was this?

What kind of house was the man operating?

People who understood such things tried to explain. They said the man was studying the motions of the heavenly bodies or something of the kind—an explanation, under the circumstances, that did more harm than good. The stolid, unimaginative farmers listened to the explanations with the mounting anger the normal mind throws up to fend off the unusual. In an age when few white men read books, and even fewer considered scientific

careers, it was worse than useless to tell people that a black man
was studying the stars. One can almost hear the peals of laughter
as the stories made the rounds. A black man studying the
motions of the heavenly bodies! Who ever heard of such
goings-on?

Before too many years had passed, the whole world had
heard of Benjamin Banneker, the first American black scholar
and the first black man of national stature to give vent to the
Negro protest. As an advocate, and as an example, Banneker
made a fundamental contribution during the formative years
of the American people. In the years of the Revolution, and
after, when Thomas Jefferson and others expressed doubts
about the mental endowment of black people, Banneker stood
out, like a rock in a raging stream, as a center of safety and truth
for blacks and whites who lost their footing and surrendered to
the deception of appearances. He preached eloquently in letters
and in private conversation against "the long-established illiberal
prejudice against the blacks." Of even more importance was the
propaganda of his deeds. As a mathematician, as an astronomer,
surveyor, poet, mechanic, philosopher, clock-maker, and zool-
ogist, Banneker startled men and made them question their
assumptions.

All over the world, at this juncture, reason followed profit;
and men, as usual, found it easy to believe what served their
pocketbooks. They believed, in other words, that black men
were phylogenetically incapable of absorbing "the wonders and
mysteries" of Western civilization. Wherever this doctrine was
preached, men had to overcome the hurdle of Banneker, who
not only beat white men at their own games but also devised
new games for white men to play. In Paris, the founders of the
Societé des Amis des Noirs discussed the phenomenon of "America's
African Astronomer." So did Pitt and Wilberforce and Buxton
in the House of Commons in London. After 1791, when
Banneker participated in the survey of Washington, D.C.,

Americans admitted his weight, though some, characteristically, looked upon him as a biological sport who proved only that it was dangerous to mix black people and alphabets.

The Banneker years and the Banneker protests were one with the founding of America. Banneker's grandfather came to America on a slave ship. But so, in a manner of speaking, did his white grandmother.

The grandmother, an extraordinary personage named Molly Welsh, was a poor English worker who ran afoul of the harsh laws regulating employers and employees. For a minor offense, she was shipped to America and sold to a planter for seven years to pay the cost of her passage. Molly Welsh, in short, was an indentured servant — as were many, perhaps most, of the first settlers.

Most white indentured servants were singularly free of racial prejudice. They worked in the fields with black slaves and black indentured servants; they shared huts and tankards of rum with blacks and they married them, even in the South. The relationship between black and white indentured servants was close in Maryland, where Molly Welsh worked out her term of servitude and acquired, by stringent economies, a small nest egg. After completing her term of service, she bought a small farm and acquired, as another token of upward mobility, two slaves from a ship in Chesapeake Bay. One of the slaves was an African of some importance who continued to worship African gods. According to tradition, he was the son of an African king. However that may be, the African in question, one Bannaky, certainly had the airs of a royal person. Or so it seemed to Molly Welsh, who worked the two slaves for a spell and then freed them. Immediately thereafter she married Bannaky and took his name, which was subsequently Anglicized to Bannaker or Banneker.

To Banneker and his English wife were born four children, only one of whom concerns us here. Mary, the oldest, followed her mother's example and married a native African, Robert, who took her name. Among their children was Benjamin Banneker, who was born on November 9, 1731. Six years later, Robert Banneker bought 102 acres in a thinly populated region near Baltimore and built a family home on the brow of a hill over-looking the Patapsco Valley.

Young Benjamin Banneker grew up in a world of ambiguity and change. The status of free Afro-Americans at that time was relatively high. They could vote, marry anyone who wanted to marry them, hold property and dispose of it. Although free Afro-Americans had a place, the place was not well-defined; it depended on a multiplicity of variables and an ingenious black man could rise by exploiting fissures in the wall.

Banneker, like his famous contemporary Phillis Wheatley, exploited and eventually transcended the wall that hemmed black people in. Like Wheatley, he was a bookworm. His grandmother taught him letters and he was soon reading the Bible. The family arranged for the precocious youngster to attend an integrated neighborhood school. With his black and white schoolmates, Banneker learned the rudiments of arith-metic, writing, and reading. Then he dropped out of school to help his father with the farm. But he was no longer the same boy. Farm work irked him now, for he had caught a vision of a larger world. He wanted books, pencil, and paper. But the little farming community near Baltimore provided few opportunities for scholars — black or white. Most of Banneker's white neigh-bors were illiterate, books were hard to come by, and learning was considered a luxury. Here and there, provisions were made for bright and well-to-do white boys. But a black scholar and scientist! Everyone — or almost everyone — knew that blacks could not learn — a "fact" that was related in some way to the color of their skin.

Perceiving the drift of the age, probing into the web of relationships that bound and separated black and white folk,

Banneker retreated within himself and made his own world. While tending cows or tilling the ground, he chewed over the basic problems he had learned in school. Within a few years, he had thoroughly digested the basic principles of mathematics. Retreating further inward, the farm boy concentrated on his senses and sensations. The whole world — the sky, the ground, the rain, the seasons — became a school to him. By the time he reached twenty, Banneker had a photographic memory and the eye and instincts of a man of science. Although he had never seen a clock, he made one, using as a model a borrowed watch. All parts of the clock, which was probably the first homemade clock in America, were chipped laboriously out of wood. Banneker's clock, which was completed about 1761, worked perfectly for more than twenty years and people came from miles around to hear it sound the hours.

By 1770, Banneker was a community celebrity. It was the fashion in this age for men of leisure to exchange difficult mathematical problems. In this game, Banneker had few peers. He often returned the answers in rhyme. His fame, as a result, leaped the bounds of Maryland. From all over Colonial America came problems and questions for the African mathematician.

But Banneker's primary problem — a vocation — remained unsolved. On the death of his father and mother, he became the sole proprietor of the farm. There are indications that the idealistic young man considered this windfall a calamity. He was appalled by the time he would have to spend away from his musings and meditations.

A stroke of fate saved the scholar from the pig pen. On the eve of the Revolutionary War, the Ellicotts, a talented and humane Quaker family, settled in the community and erected a flour mill. Three sons of this distinguished family were mathematicians and astronomers of note. They immediately perceived what their duller peers missed: that Banneker was a man of unusual talents. George Ellicott gave Banneker three books, Mayer's *Tables*, Ferguson's *Astronomy*, Leadbetter's *Lunar Tables*, and some astronomical instruments. The Ellicotts also solved Banneker's domestic problems. In return for an annuity of twelve pounds, and a life interest in the farm, Banneker conveyed his property to his white friends.

Freed now from cows and corn, with leisure for contemplation and books for study, Banneker gave himself up to scholarly pursuits. Astronomy became the burning passion of his life. Within a few years, he could predict eclipses. In 1791, he completed calculations for his first almanac, which was published in 1792.

James McHenry, a prominent Baltimore politician who later served as secretary of war, helped Banneker find a publisher for the almanac. In a letter to Goddard & Angel, the Baltimore publishers, he underlined Banneker's importance as an advocate in the flesh. "I consider this Negro as fresh proof that the powers of the mind are disconnected with the color of the skin, or, in other words, a striking contrast to Mr. Hume's doctrine, that 'the Negroes are naturally inferior to the whites, and unsusceptible of attainments in arts and sciences.' In every civilized country, we shall find thousands of whites liberally educated and who have enjoyed greater opportunities for instruction than this Negro, his inferiors in those intellectual acquirements and capacities that form the most characteristic features in the human race."

McHenry was one of several powerful whites who came within the orbit of Banneker's influence. In his dealings with men of substance, Banneker was artful in his advocacy of the Afro-American's cause. He always urged upon his friends the emancipation of slaves and the elevation of free Negroes. To deprive Afro-Americans of ambition and hope, he said, was to rob them of the credentials of manhood.

Another influential friend, Major Andrew Ellicott, succeeded in getting Banneker appointed to the commission that laid out the city of Washington, D.C. With the approval of George Washington, Banneker and Ellicott were named to assist Pierre Charles L'Enfant, the brilliant and temperamental French engineer who conceived and drew up the original plan for the ten-mile-square area set aside for the nation's Capital. The naming of Banneker to the Capital commission marked the first presidential appointment received by a Negro.

The African astronomer accompanied Ellicott and L'Enfant to Washington and shared in the deliberations and computations of the commission. The *Georgetown Weekly Ledger* of March 12, 1791, noted the arrival of L'Enfant and Ellicott, who were "attended by Benjamin Banneker, an Ethiopian, whose abilities as surveyor and astronomer already prove that Mr. Jefferson's concluding that that race of men were void of mental endowment, was without foundation."

L'Enfant was the moving spirit behind the Washington plan. With Ellicott and Banneker assisting, he laid out a show city with great avenues and vistas and open spaces. When a major property owner and political power erected a mansion that obstructed one of his vistas, L'Enfant, the temperamental artist, immediately tore it down. Washington reluctantly dismissed him, and L'Enfant departed in a huff, leaving the calculations to Ellicott and Banneker.

In the middle of 1791, Banneker returned to his home near Baltimore. He was now fifty-five, and he was the best known black man in America. Invitations were pressed upon him from all quarters and strangers beat a path to his farm. On a favorite horse, Banneker made the rounds and related his experiences in Washington. People who had ridiculed him for wasting his time now gathered close to hear words from his lips. Sitting in the middle of a group in the combination post office and store, leaning on his staff, Banneker told his neighbors of the currents at work in the outside world. Of medium stature, running to fat around the middle, white-haired, pleasant-miened, with dreamy, otherworldly eyes, the county celebrity made a noble appearance. He dressed in "superfine broadcloth" cut in the current mode: a plain coat with straight collar and long waistcoat topped by a broad-brimmed hat.

By all standards, Banneker should have been the happiest of men. His work was going well. Scholars had acclaimed his dissertation on bees and a study which proved that the locust plague recurred in seventeen-year cycles. Now, in the middle of 1791, publishers were bringing out his first almanac. It is true that he had no family. But he seemed to prefer it that way. With no wife, with no responsibilities, he was free to study stars at night and sleep during the day. In his spare time, he washed his own clothes, cooked his own food and corresponded with scholars. For relaxation, he sat under a huge chestnut tree in his orchard and played the flute or the violin. He was famous, free, and comparatively well-to-do. What else could he want?

There was something. Banneker had returned from Washington with a sense of impending doom. The winds of change were blowing in the new nation called America, and they were blowing the Afro-American no good. Banneker concluded that the wave of revolutionary idealism in America had reached its peak. The great tide of interracial amity that followed the Revolutionary War was receding, leaving in its wake fear and hate and anxiety. All about him were signs. Free black men were being hemmed in by restrictions and oppressive rules: they were insulted on the streets, barred from employment, and proscribed in the church. Laws were being devised that stripped slaves of every vestige of human personality. Walls — walls of hate and fear and guilt — were closing off every avenue of black advancement. In Banneker's youth, it had been possible for blacks and whites to marry. He himself had attended an integrated school. Now, a scant fifty years later, these things were no longer possible. There were 757,000 black people in America, two out of every ten persons. Of this number, 59,000 were free. But the differences between slaves and free Afro-Americans were being flattened out and obscured. It seemed almost that men feared free Afro-Americans more than they feared slaves. Something, Banneker told himself—something must be done. Why, he wondered, didn't the Afro-American's friends speak out? A word at this critical juncture, when the moulds of a nation and a people were being poured—a word now could make a great deal of difference.

Banneker's mind turned to Thomas Jefferson, who was the great and brooding symbol of the age. Jefferson had, when his blood was hot, championed emancipation and manumission of slaves. In a burst of revolutionary idealism, he had written: "All men are created equal." But Jefferson was not the first, nor the last, to set down words that frightened him. As the years wore on, as the black population increased, Jefferson hedged his bet with polysyllabic rationalizations. He had not disowned the Declaration of Independence. But he seemed to be saying now that white men were created more equal than black people. And worse: he had not manumitted the hundred or more slaves he held at Monticello. Thinking about these things, following the eddies and currents of the age, Banneker decided that the time was ripe for an act. There had been individual acts of protest in Boston and Philadelphia, but these protests were muted. Free Afro-Americans claimed, with good cause, that their lifelines were too exposed to make an open protest. Banneker proposed to abandon caution and speak openly—as a man. To whom? To Thomas Jefferson, of course. Banneker gathered the manuscript pages of his first almanac and sat down at the oval table in his living room. Dipping pen in ink, he put down these words:

MARYLAND, BALTIMORE COUNTY,
August 19, 1791

SIR,

I am fully sensible of the greatness of the freedom I take with you on the present occasion; a liberty which seemed to me scarcely allowable, when I reflected on that distinguished and dignified station in which you stand, and the almost general prejudice and prepossession, which is so prevalent in the world against those of my complexion.

I suppose it is a truth too well attested to you, to need a proof here, that we are a race of beings, who have long laboured under the abuse and censure of the world; that we have long been looked upon with an eye of contempt; and that we have long been considered rather as brutish than human, and scarcely capable of mental endowments.

Sir, I hope I may safely admit, in consequence of the report which has reached me, that you are a man less inflexible in sentiments of this nature, than many others; that you are measurably friendly, and well disposed towards us; and that you are willing and ready to lend your aid and assistance to our relief, from those many distresses, and numerous calamities, to which we are reduced.

Now Sir, if this is founded in truth, I apprehend you will embrace every opportunity, to eradicate that train of absurd and false ideas and opinions, which so generally prevail with respect to us; and that your sentiments are concurrent with mine, which are, that one universal Father hath given being to us all; and that He hath not only made us all of one flesh, but that He hath also, without partiality, afforded us all the same sensations, and endowed us all with the same faculties; and that however variable we may be in society or religion, however diversified in situation or colour, we are all of the same family, and stand in the same relation to Him.

Sir, if these are sentiments of which you are fully persuaded, I hope you cannot but acknowledge, that it is the indispensable duty of those, who maintain for themselves the rights of human nature, and who profess the obligations of Christianity, to extend their power and influence to the relief of every part of the human race, from whatever burden of oppression they may unjustly labour under....

Sir, I freely and cheerfully acknowledge, that I am of the African race, and in that colour which is natural to them, of the deepest dye; and it is under a sense of the most profound gratitude to the Supreme Ruler of the Universe, that I now confess to you, that I am not under that state of tyrannical thralldom, and inhuman captivity, to which too many of my brethren are doomed, but that I have abundantly tasted of the fruition of those blessings, which proceeded from that free and unequalled liberty with which you are favoured; and which, I hope, you will willingly allow you have mercifully received, from the immediate hand of that Being from whom proceedeth every good and perfect gift.

Sir, suffer me to recall to your mind that time, in which the arms and tyranny of the British crown were exerted, with every powerful effort, in order to reduce you to a state of servitude; look back, I entreat you, on the variety of dangers to which you were exposed; reflect on that time, in which every human aid appeared unavailable ... and you cannot but be led to a serious and grateful sense of your miraculous and providential preservation. ...

This, Sir, was a time when you clearly saw into the injustice of a state of slavery, and in which you had just apprehensions of the horrors of its condition. It was then that your abhorrence thereof was so excited that you publicly held forth this true and invaluable doctrine, which is worthy to be recorded and remembered in all succeeding ages: "We hold these truths to be self-evident, that all men are created equal; that they are endowed by their Creator with certain inalienable rights, and that among these are life, liberty, and the pursuit of happiness."

Here was a time, in which your tender feelings for yourselves had engaged you thus to declare; you were then impressed with proper ideas of the great violation of liberty, and the free possession of those blessings, to which you were entitled by nature; but, sir, how pitiable it is to reflect, that although you were so fully convinced of the benevolence of the Father of Mankind, and of His equal and impartial distribution of these rights and privileges, which He hath conferred upon them, that you should at the same time counteract His mercies, in detaining by fraud and violence, so numerous a part of my brethren under groaning captivity, and cruel oppression, that you should at the same time be found guilty of that most criminal act, which you professedly detested in others, with respect to yourselves.

I suppose that your knowledge of the situation of my brethren is too extensive to need a recital here; neither shall I presume to prescribe methods by which they may be relieved, otherwise than by recommending to you and all others, to wean yourself from those narrow prejudices which you have imbibed with respect to them, and as Job proposed to his friends, "put your soul in their soul's stead"; thus shall your hearts be enlarged with kindness and benevolence towards them; and thus shall you need neither the direction of myself or others, in what manners to proceed herein.

Banneker stopped and reread his lines. Perhaps he had been too bold. After all, it was not the custom for black people to speak thus to white people. It was certainly not customary for black people to speak frankly to a man of Jefferson's stature. Banneker thought for a moment and then added a modest and clever disclaimer.

And now, Sir, although my sympathy and affection for my brethren has caused my enlargement thus far, I ardently hope that your candour and generosity will plead with you in my behalf, when I make known to you that it was not originally my design; but having taken up my pen in order to direct to you, as a present, a copy of an Almanac which I have calculated for the succeeding year, I was unexpectedly and unavoidably led thereto.

This calculation is the product of my arduous study, in this my advanced stage of life....I have taken the liberty to direct a copy to you which I humbly request you will favourably receive and although you may have the opportunity of perusing it after its publication, yet I desire to send it to you in manuscript previous thereto, thereby you might not only have an earlier inspection, but that you might also view it in my own handwriting.

And now, Sir, I shall conclude, and subscribe myself, with the most profound respect.

Your most obedient humble servant,
Benjamin Banneker

The letter reached Jefferson, who was then secretary of state in George Washington's cabinet, at Philadelphia. Jefferson's immediate impressions are not a matter of record. Over the next decade, he said various things about Benjamin Banneker, some of them quite harsh. But to Banneker himself he presented his best face in reply.

Philadelphia, Aug. 30, 1791

Sir,

I thank you most sincerely, for your letter of the 19th instant, and for the Almanac it contained. Nobody wishes more than I do, to see such proofs as you exhibit, that nature has given to our black brethren talents equal to those of the other color of men; and that the appearance of the want of them is owing merely to the degraded condition of their existence, both in Africa and America. I can add with truth, that nobody wishes more ardently to see a good system commenced, for raising the condition, both of their body and mind, to what it ought to be, as far as the imbecility of their present existence, and other circumstances, which cannot be neglected, will admit.

I have taken the liberty of sending your Almanac to Monsieur de Condorcet, Secretary of the Academy of Sciences, at Paris, and Member of the Philanthropic Society, because I considered it as a document to which your whole colour have a right for their justification against the doubts which have been entertained of them.

> I am, with great esteem, Sir,
> Your most obedient humble servant,
> THO. JEFFERSON

MR. BENJAMIN BANNEKER, near
ELLICOT'S LOWER MILLS, BALTIMORE COUNTY.

Banneker's letter and Jefferson's answer made a big ripple in the events of the day. The correspondence was discussed in France, England, and the South. But nothing happened. Slavery continued its ominous march across the soul of America. Frightened by the successful Haitian Revolution and abortive slave revolts in Virginia and other states, masters elaborated increasingly severe rules for the control of slaves and free Afro-Americans.

In dwindling hope, then, and with foreboding for the country he loved, Banneker lived out his measured days. A gentle, Christian man who never joined a church, he turned in his winter days to the advocacy of peace. His plan for *A Lasting Peace* anticipated many of the principles of the League of Nations and the United Nations. But neither in peace nor in tolerance did he overcome. The whole drift of the age was against him. Wars and rumors of wars and the clanking of slave chains: these things were in the wind in October, 1806. Banneker was resting in his home one day in that month when he seemed to hear voices beckoning him to another world. On an impulse, he rose and started down the path leading from his house. He had not gone far when his strength gave out and he sank helplessly to the ground. He died later that day and was buried in an unmarked grave. But the idea the gentle scholar and advocate symbolized could not be disposed of so easily. Within twenty years, Banneker was disturbing the peace of racists from the grave. His name and his letter ("Look back, I entreat you") were cited repeatedly by abolitionists in their successful assault on the intellectual props of the slave South. Banneker has been no less

The Stargazer

persuasive in our own times. For men who dare and dream, for men who appeal from the gutters to the stars, for men who stand up and protest, no matter what the odds, the stargazer remains a persuasive and articulate example.

COLONIAL CATALYST

---◆---

Prince Hall

*Fellow-citizens, let us entreat you, have faith
in your own principles. If freedom is good for
any, it is good for all.*

ADDRESS OF COLORED NATIONAL
CONVENTION, 1864

PRINCE HALL

THE COLONIES WERE ablaze with indignation. In Virginia, Patrick Henry was speaking of liberty or death. In New York and South Carolina, in Rhode Island and Maryland, Sons of Liberty were demonstrating and boycotting. Boston, the center of colonial discontent, was a festering boil of boycotts, processions, and bonfires. An unruly crowd of black laborers, white artisans, seamen and mechanics virtually controlled Boston streets. Business was at a standstill. Stores, offices, even courts, were closed. Night after night, men poured from garrets and taverns, screaming, "No taxation without representation."

Moving along the edge of the tumultuous Boston crowds was a thin, delicate-looking teenager. His name was Prince Hall and he had just arrived from Barbados, where he had been born about 1748, the son of an Englishman and a free black woman. Hall was, in theory, free; but he was also a black man and he knew that neither in Boston nor in Barbados were black men free in fact. As the revolutionary drama swirled in the streets before him, Prince Hall wondered what it all meant to Puritan slaveholders. He wondered if they were sincere and if it had occurred to them that every principle from which they acted was "stronger than a thousand arguments in favor" of black people and slaves.

The audacity, the sheer effrontery, of American patriots fascinated Hall. The colonists held in servitude more than a half million human beings, some of them white; yet they proposed to go to war in support of the theory that all men were created equal. In 1765, when Hall worked his way to Boston on a ship, there were almost sixteen thousand black people in New England—almost all of them slaves and social pariahs. Prince Hall moved around Boston with his eyes open and he was appalled by the social and economic conditions of slaves and free Afro-Americans. Even more appalling to the sensitive youth was the indifference of colonial patriots. Boston, at that time, was a center of the American slave trade. In one way or another, most men of substance benefited from the trade in men and the ancillary businesses that grew up around it. Most of the major leaders of the revolutionary movement, in fact, were slaveholders or investors in slave-supported businesses. What did these men mean by freedom?

Not only Hall but thousands of other Americans were disturbed by this question. Tom Paine, James Otis, Abigail Adams and other revolutionary leaders told the colonists that their pretensions were inconsistent with their practices. Patrick Henry, an honest slaveholder, admitted that slavery was wrong but said he was "drawn along by the general inconvenience of living without them [slaves]."

What of the slaves and the free Afro-Americans?

What did the revolutionary agitation mean to them?

Prince Hall investigated the wharves and alleys where un-attached Afro-Americans lived. He listened to their discussions and their arguments and noted, with approval, the rapid growth of political and social consciousness. There had been individual protests and collective revolts, as Prince Hall knew. But free Afro-Americans had been strangely silent. Now, as Hall watched, the ghetto came alive. For the first time in America, for the first time anywhere, city Afro-Americans found a voice and a technique. Slave revolts and underground resistance had taken place outside the system. Afro-Americans proposed now to use the ideology and instruments of the system to smash the system. They proposed to bore from within and destroy legal forms with legal forms. Their first technique, one that would reach full flower 194 years later, was legal contention.

In the 1760's, Prince Hall watched with burning interest as the black soul expanded and made its first tentative probes in enemy territory. As early as 1766, one year after Hall's arrival, Boston Afro-Americans filed a test case against slavery. The movement spread to Connecticut and other states. Under the leadership of men whose names were not recorded, slaves and free men collected money, hired lawyers, and filed suits, asking for freedom and damages for unlawful detention. In Connecticut and Massachusetts, slave-instigated suits were appealed to the highest courts. In some courts, judges granted the pleas of slave petitioners.

Afro-Americans, in this period, also experimented with mass pressure. Meetings were held, petitions for freedom were circulated and signed. Courts and legislatures were bombarded with petitions from Americans protesting tyranny and oppression in America.

Ingenious men found other ways to turn the revolutionary turmoil to their advantage. Some black men, like Crispus Attucks, the leader of the crowd in the Boston Massacre, appropriated American slogans and assumed leadership in the street riots in Boston and other cities. Still others, more cynical or more realistic, sided with the British. As the agitation intensified, slaves and free men became bolder. The number of slave escapes increased sharply, the number of incidents multiplied.

The first wave of agitation unfolded without conscious planning or direction. In the 1770's, however, self-conscious men who considered themselves leaders and were so considered by others stepped from the anonymity of the crowd and assumed control of men and events. Among the most talented of these pioneer leaders was Prince Hall, who had moved for six or

seven years on the edge of events, studying men and organizations. Hall spent his first years in Boston in study and hard
work. Working as a laborer in the day and studying at night, he
saved enough money to buy property. He also became a
Methodist minister and a talented organizer and advocate of
freedom. Within ten years of his arrival in Boston, the young
man from Barbados was one of the leading lights of the first
Freedom movement.

As one of America's first abolitionists, Hall made a big
contribution to the movement that led to the erosion of slavery
in the North. As organizer and leader of the first black organization outside the black church, Hall also made an important
contribution to the development of black morale and solidarity.

Hall excelled in the areas of organization and technique.
During the first wave of agitation, he learned the value of an
organizational base. And he was soon preaching the virtues of
solidarity and collective action to the scattered and largely
demoralized black population of Boston. Though free, Hall
made a point of signing slave petitions, an act that dramatized
the unity of fate of free blacks and slaves.

His major contribution, however, was the organization of the
first black Masonic lodge. He attempted first to enter a lodge of
the white American Masons. Rebuffed, he applied to a lodge
attached to a British regiment stationed near Boston. On March
6, 1775, Prince Hall and fourteen other black men were initiated
into Masonry in the British Army lodge. When the British
regiment withdrew, the black Masons formed, under a limited
permit, African Lodge No. 1, one of the first black organizations
in America. After the war, Hall was granted a charter from the
Grand Lodge of England. On May 6, 1787, African Lodge No.
459 was formally organized in Boston with Hall as master. This
event, coming less than a month after the founding of the Free
African Society of Philadelphia, was an epochal leap forward
in black consciousness. In 1797, Hall helped organize African

lodges in Philadelphia and Providence, Rhode Island, thereby becoming a pioneer in the development of a black interstate organization.

Throughout this period, Hall protested bigotry and discrimination. Like most Afro-Americans, he fought on two fronts in the Revolutionary War. As an American patriot and a soldier in George Washington's army, Hall opposed British tyranny. As a black man, he opposed American bigots with their own weapons: the lofty words of the Declaration of Independence. With many other Afro-Americans, Hall saw service on Bunker Hill. When George Washington arrived to take command of the Army of Cambridge, he found scores of black men in the ranks. Although these veterans had fought with distinction at Lexington, Concord, and Bunker Hill, Washington immediately barred them from the Continental Army. The Afro-Americans of New England refused to accept this blow without protest. Hall, according to tradition, led a delegation of free Afro-Americans who took their complaints to Washington's headquarters. Washington was impressed by the delegation's plea. Hall and his group were too diplomatic and clever to show all their cards, but they managed somehow to convey a subtle threat.

The colonists, at that moment, were pressed on all sides. They lacked manpower and weapons. To make matters worse, an uncomfortably large number of Americans were siding with Great Britain. In this volatile situation, America could ill afford additional enemies. Lord Dunmore made this abundantly clear when he issued a proclamation welcoming slaves and free Afro-Americans to the British Army. Thousands of slaves, including some who belonged to Thomas Jefferson and George Washington, abandoned the plantations to fight for their own freedom. Apprised of these developments, George Washington overruled himself and countenanced the enlistment of free Afro-Americans who had served in the army at Cambridge.

In a letter to the president of Congress, Washington explained his decision. Said he: "It has been presented to me, that the free Negroes, who have served in this army, are very much dissatisfied at being discarded. As it is to be apprehended, that they may seek employ in the ministerial [British] army, I have presumed to depart from the resolution respecting them, and have given license for their being enlisted . . ." After the disastrous winter of Valley Forge, Washington scrapped all resolutions and accepted free Negroes and slaves.

Prince Hall and other black leaders continued to trouble the soul of America during the war years. In pamphlets and petitions, they stressed the close connection between American freedom and black freedom. Hall was the moving force behind a "slave petition" that openly questioned the sincerity and the good sense of American patriots. This petition, which was filed on January 13, 1777, with the General Court of Massachusetts, is reproduced, in part, below:

The petition of a great number of Negroes, who are detained in a state of slavery in the very bowels of a free and Christian country, humbly showing,—

That your petitioners apprehend that they have, in common with all other men, a natural and inalienable right to that freedom, which the great Parent of the universe hath bestowed equally on all mankind, and which they have never forfeited by any compact or agreement whatever. But they were unjustly dragged by the cruel hand of power from their dearest friends, and some of them even torn from the embraces of their tender parents,—from a populous, pleasant and plentiful country, and in violation of the laws of nature and of nations, and in defiance of all the tender feelings of humanity, brought hither to be sold like beasts of burthen, and like them, condemned to slavery for life—among a people possessing the mild religion of Jesus—a people not insensible of the sweets of national freedom, nor without a spirit to resent the unjust endeavors of others to reduce them to a state of bondage and subjection . . .

[The petitioners] cannot but express astonishment that it has never been considered, that every principle from which America has acted, in the course of her unhappy difficulties with Great Britain, bears stronger than a thousand arguments in favor of your humble petitioners. They therefore humbly beseech Your Honors to give their petition its due weight and consideration, and cause an act of the legislature to be passed, whereby they may be restored to the enjoyment of that freedom, which is the natural right of all men, and their children (who were born in the land of liberty) may not be held as slaves after they arrive at the age of twenty-one years. So may the inhabitants of this State (no longer chargeable with the inconsistency of acting themselves the part which they condemn and oppose in others) be prospered in their glorious struggles for liberty, and have those blessings secured to them by Heaven, of which benevolent minds cannot wish to deprive their fellowmen.

And your petitioners, as in duty bound, shall ever pray:———

LANCASTER HILL,
PETER BESS,
BRISTEN SLENFEN,
PRINCE HALL,
JACK PIERPONT, [his X mark]
NERO FUNELO, [his X mark]
NEWPORT SUMNER, [his X mark]

Also active during this period were Hall's contemporaries, Phillis Wheatley and Paul Cuffe. Wheatley, the second American woman to publish a book, did not voice open protests, but she struck blows for the cause with her poems. Cuffe, a wealthy captain who sailed his own ships to Europe and Africa, was out-spoken and inventive. Barred from the ballot box in Dartmouth, Massachusetts, he refused to pay taxes and filed a defiant petition of protest. After a long controversy it was decided that taxation without representation in America was tyranny. The case was widely regarded as establishing a precedent for black suffrage.

After the war, the Freedom movement continued with assaults on the slave trade and the Afro-American's perennial issue, equal education. By this time, Hall was known throughout New England as a skillful user of the public petition. In 1787, he filed one of the first public petitions for equal education. He later asked the selectmen of Boston to establish a school house for black children. Education, to Hall, was a key to power.

"We . . . must fear for our rising offspring," he said, "to see them in ignorance in a land of gospel light, when there is provision made for them as well as others and yet [they] can't enjoy them, and [no other reason] can be given [than that] they are black . . ."

Hall also took the lead in antislavery agitation. When three black men were kidnapped and sold into slavery in the West Indies, Hall sprang into action. Under his leadership, black people filed an antislavery petition with the Massachusetts legislature. Spurred on by the petition, Governor John Hancock filed an official protest. The three men were located and returned to Boston, where a huge celebration was held. This incident and the protest of blacks and whites led to the passage of a state law against the slave trade.

Despite isolated gains, this was a difficult period for the Afro-Americans. In the first flush of victory, there was a rash of manumissions. Other Afro-Americans received freedom as a result of war service, court suits or legislative action. By 1790, slavery was a dying institution in the North.

Not all men rejoiced.

To poor whites, the recently emancipated slaves were an economic threat. To aristocrats and businessmen, free blacks were social dynamite, an anomalous group in a social system designed for two: slaves and free white men. With one eye on the Haitian Revolution, which began in 1791, and another on the sharp upswing in the free black population in towns and cities, men of power began enacting discriminatory legislation. The freedom of black people was severely restricted. They could not walk on the streets of Boston after 9 P.M. without a pass; they could not go outside the bounds of their community without a pass. They could not own certain types of property. Worse, they were barred from the best jobs. In Boston, in the turbulent years after the Revolution, free black men were insulted, threatened, and beaten by mobs of poor whites. On public occasions, they were barred from Boston Common.

Prince Hall

Prince Hall watched the darkening clouds with deepening despair. The old patriot was especially horrified by the desecration of the symbols of the Revolution. On July 4th, public-spirited crowds celebrated the birth of the Republic by whipping Negroes and driving them from the streets of Boston.

Particularly shocking was an incident involving one Colonel Middleton, a hard-swearing, hard-fighting black man who had commanded a black company in the Revolutionary War. Prince Hall was doubtless aware of the Boston riot described by Lydia Maria Childs, who witnessed it as a child. "About three o'clock in the afternoon," she wrote, "shouts of a beginning fray reached us. Soon, terrified children and women ran down Belknap street, pursued by white boys, who enjoyed their fright. The sounds of battle approached; clubs and brickbats were flying in all directions. At this crisis, Col. Middleton opened his door, armed with a loaded musket, and, in a loud voice, shrieked death to the first white men who should approach. Hundreds of human beings, white and black, were pouring down the streets, the blacks making but a feeble resistance, the odds in numbers and spirit being against them. Col. Middleton's voice could be heard above every other, urging his party to turn and resist to the last. His appearance was terrific, his musket was levelled, ready to sacrifice the first white man that came within its range. The colored party, shamed by his reproaches, and fired by his example, rallied, and made a short show of resistance."

Lydia Maria Child's father approached Colonel Middleton and asked him to put away his gun. The colonel stood for a while in defiance, then said: "I will do it for you, for you have always been kind to me." So saying, the old black soldier retired from the scene, weeping and cursing as he went.

That men who had risked life and limb should be treated so grieved Prince Hall. To be sure, Hall himself was not personally affected by the climate of creeping bigotry. He and his second wife (his first wife died in 1769) had a comfortable and well-appointed home. They had no children, but they had a wide circle of friends; and their home in Lendell's Lane was a windbreak against the gathering storm.

As a soap manufacturer and artisan, Hall had accumulated money and property. As a minister and grand master in the Masonic order, he was a man of weight and substance in the community. White men of power considered him something of an exception, a patronizing attitude that Hall neither encouraged nor accepted.

A slight man of small stature with brooding good looks, fair skin and commanding eyes, Hall was reasonably happy and content. Still, he feared for the future of his people. And he raised his voice in rebuke and remonstrance. It seemed to some, and it must have seemed sometimes to Hall himself, that he was tilting at windmills. But he continued to speak out, demanding for black men not only freedom but the full credentials of citizenship: social, political, and economic equality. Hall's hope, faith, and forbearance did not find an echo in the hearts of "stand-and-shoot" men like Colonel Middleton. But his insistence on full equality raised the consciousness of many of his contemporaries.

Until his death on Friday, November 4, 1807, Hall championed the twin interests of his life: organizational effectiveness and human brotherhood. His charge to the African Lodge, delivered at Menotomy (now West Cambridge) on June 24, 1797, was a requiem to the death of a dream stillborn. But it was also an extraordinary leap of faith in one of the Afro-American's worst hours. Hall began with a doleful recitation of woes and tribulations.

"...let us see our friends and brethren; and first let us see them dragged from their native country, by the iron hand of tyranny and oppression, from their dear friends and connections, with weeping eyes and aching hearts, to a strange land, and among a strange people, whose tender mercies are cruel,—

and there to bear the iron yoke of slavery and cruelty, till death, as a friend, shall relieve them. And must not the unhappy condition of these, our fellowmen, draw forth our hearty prayers and wishes for their deliverance from those merchants and traders. . . .

"Now, my brethren, as we see and experience, that all things here are frail and changeable and nothing here to be depended upon: Let us seek those things which are above, and at the same time let us pray to Almighty God, while we remain in the tabernacle, that he would give us the grace of patience and strength to bear up under all our troubles, which at this day God knows we have our share. Patience, I say, for were we not possessed of a great measure of it, you could not bear up under the daily insults you meet with in the streets of Boston; much more on public days of recreation, how are you shamefully abused, and that at such a degree, that you may truly be said to carry your lives in your hands; and the arrows of death are flying about your heads; helpless old women have their clothes torn off their backs, even to the exposing of their nakedness. . . ."

What then was to be done?

Hall was honest; he had no easy answers. The tentacles of slavery were penetrating the private places of every man's soul and it seemed, in this white hour, that slavery would never die. But this, Hall said, was the deception of appearances "for the darkest hour is just before the break of day." Hall urged his listeners to persevere. He reminded them of the unexpected successes of the Haitian Revolution and concluded with a Jubilee for the day when men would receive men as friends and treat them as brothers.

Even as Hall spoke, storm clouds were gathering that would give meaning to his years of pioneering protest and his ringing affirmation of hope: "Thus does Ethiopia stretch forth her hand from slavery to freedom and equality."

GOD *and* BLACK POWER

Richard Allen

> *If you love your children, if you love your country, if you love the God of love, clear your hands from slaves, burden not your children or country with them.*
>
> **RICHARD ALLEN**

RICHARD ALLEN

WHEN THE LITTLE BAND of black Christians arrived at St. George's Methodist Episcopal Church, the sexton pointed to the gallery. The black men paused and then ascended the rickety stairs with downcast eyes and heavy hearts. To Richard Allen and Absalom Jones, the leaders of the group, this was the ultimate indignity—to be shunted from the first floor to the gallery in a Christian church black men had helped to build. God, Richard Allen recalled, had promised to prepare a place for all his children. But was this the place?

Richard Allen did not think so. His mind ran over the thousand insults offered black men in Christian churches and he remembered that it was not always so. In the old days, before the Revolution, black and white Methodists had praised God together on their knees; they had shared love feasts and had visited in each other's homes. And now this! What was behind it? Richard Allen did not know. He imagined that the sudden increase in the number of black worshippers had some-thing to do with it—that and the spirit of bigotry which was creeping across the land. How else could he account for the recent changes in church policy—the rule that confined black men to the back seat of the first floor and the shameful custom that required black people to wait until all white people had partaken of the blood and body of Christ? And now, on a Sunday in November, 1796, church leaders were making good on their threat to banish Negroes to the second floor — a little closer, the more cynical said, to heaven. Richard Allen shook his head in doubt and despair. But he refused to doubt God. Men — little men with little minds — were responsible for this desecration of His house of worship.

A voice broke into Allen's reverie. "Let us pray," said the elder, indicating the beginning of the Sunday service. Without thinking, Allen and the little band of black men plopped down where they were — in the *front* of the gallery. Allen was praying as hard as he could when he heard loud voices and scuffling. What was this? Allen looked up and his blood grew cold. The white sexton was trying to pull Absalom Jones from his knees.

"You must get up; you must not kneel down here!" the sexton said.

"Wait until the prayer is over," Absalom Jones replied, pushing himself to the floor.

"No," the sexton said, pulling on Jones' arm. "No, you must get up now, or I will call for aid and force you away."

The voices echoed through the church in a weird counterpoint to the prayer of the elder. Heads shot up and startled eyes beheld the incredible scene of the black Christian and the white Christian wrestling over the meaning of God's word.

"Get up!" the sexton said. "Get up!"

"Wait until the prayer is over," Jones replied wearily. "Wait until the prayer is over and I will not trouble you any more."

The sexton called for help. Several white Christians responded and the struggle spread over the gallery. Before the white men could pull the black men from their knees, the prayer had ended. The black men stood up then and, without a word, streamed out of the church. Richard Allen added a mournful amen — "*. . . and they were no more plagued by us in the church.*"

White people were no more plagued by black people in thousands of churches. For the Philadelphia incident — the first nonviolent public demonstration by free Afro-Americans —was a focal point in a national protest movement. Without concert, without conscious planning, black people in cities in the North and South walked out of white churches and established their own institutions. The movement, which began during the Revolutionary War, marked a fundamental turning point in the relationship of black men to America. Black men everywhere were lifted up and exalted by the revolutionary rhetoric of the Declaration of Independence. When it turned out that the words had no relevance *to their lives*, they were dashed down and discomfited. It would happen again—many times. But they had no experience then with betrayal. So black people turned around within themselves and asked disturbing questions. Were they not Americans, too? And if they were not, then who, in God's name, were they? And how could they sing the Lord's song in a land that called them strangers?

Out of these questions came a new being, the American Negro, or, to be more precise, the African-American, for all of the first Negro institutions bore the interesting prefix, African. The first institutions for Afro-Americans were African Baptist churches in South Carolina, Virginia, and Georgia. George Liele and Andrew Bryan were among the pioneers in this movement, which crossed the Mason-Dixon line in the postwar period. Thomas Paul and Josiah Bishop helped establish Baptist churches in the North, including the Abyssinian Baptist Church. James Varick and Christopher Rush were among the leaders of the African Methodist Episcopal Zion Church, which was organized by a group of New Yorkers. By 1830, there were black churches of almost every conceivable denomination, including an Ethiopian Church of Jesus Christ in Savannah and a black Dutch Reformed Church in New York City.

It is impossible to overestimate the importance of this movement. One could almost say that it marked the birth of Afro-Americans as a group. Institutions are indispensable for organized social life: they are great social pools in which men see themselves and their ideals reflected. Without meetings, without rituals, ceremonies, myths and symbols, there can be no great people. Afro-Americans, recognizing this, attempted first to enter institutions formed for Americans — and were rebuffed. They then went out into the alleys and the fields and formed their own institutions and, in the process, invented themselves.

Richard Allen, the founder of the African Methodist Episcopal Church, was a germinal figure in the separate church movement. He was not, as we have seen, the originator of the movement, but he came in time to symbolize certain values created in that struggle: the importance of collective action on the part of Afro-Americans and the defiant assertion, backed up by action, that Afro-Americans would not accept a subordinate role in any American organization. Allen's point — and it is still revolutionary — was a point of power. He demanded not only the right of participation in American organizations, he also demanded the right to share in the governing of those organizations.

There is some exaggeration in Vernon Loggin's nomination of Allen for the title, "Father of the Negro," but the exaggeration contains a core of truth. John W. Cromwell, an independent investigator, said Allen "had greater influence upon the colored people of the North than any other man of his times." He was the first national black leader, a pioneer black abolitionist and the organizer and first president of the first black convention held in the Western world.

There was nothing in Allen's early life to foretell his later eminence. He was born a slave on February 14, 1760, in Philadelphia, the son, it is said, of a "pure African" father and a mulatto mother. At an early age, he was sold with his family to a white man named Stokely who owned a plantation near Dover, Delaware. Stokely was, by all accounts, a "kind" master, but Allen perceived that the evil of slavery was not in the personal relationship between master and slave but in the idea that one man could own, hold, and sell another human being. This fact was etched into Allen's soul on the day his mother and three of his brothers and sisters were sold to another master.

Allen was, by this time, a stubborn youth. He saw himself in the prism of slavery and he was, in his own words, "poor, wretched, and undone." Was there no way out? Was there no balm for black souls?

Allen asked himself these questions in the privacy of the forest where he went to study Methodism. One day — when he was about seventeen — he experienced a cataclysmic conversion that changed the contours of his life. "I went," he wrote, "with my head bowed for many days. My sins were a heavy burden. I was tempted to believe that there was no mercy for me. I cried to the Lord both night and day. One night I thought hell would be my portion. I cried unto him who delighteth to hear the prayers of a poor sinner, and, all of a sudden, my dungeon shook, my chains fell off, and 'Glory to God' I cried."

With renewed confidence and a soul filled with fire, Allen went forth to face the world, armed now with the conviction that before God there was neither black nor white, Jew nor Gentile. He began his career with an act of extraordinary symbolic significance: he helped convert his master. And his master's conversion, as the shrewd slave perhaps foresaw, led directly to his own freedom. Having heard the word of God ("Thou art weighed in the balance and art found wanting"), Stokely permitted Allen and his brothers to hire themselves out. After three years of cutting cordwood and baking brick, Allen amassed the two thousand dollars (in depreciated currency) that unlocked the door of his earthly dungeon. He went forth then as a strolling minister, walking across Pennsylvania, New

Jersey, and Maryland, pausing here and there to earn his bread at manual labor, preaching everywhere, to black and white, the good news of the gospel.

He stopped from time to time with white Methodists who extended him every courtesy. On one occasion, he sought rest, after a long walk, in the home of a white Pennsylvania couple. Completely exhausted, he collapsed before the fire. The couple invited him to dinner, but he declined. "I told them," he recalled, "that I would accept their kind invitation, but my feet pained me so I could not come to the table." The white Christian and his wife carried the table to Allen and, kneeling, bathed his feet with warm water and bran.

Allen, a devout Methodist, attended the pioneer Methodist Episcopal Conference in Baltimore in December, 1784. He was dismayed, however, by some of the decisions of the white divines. Particularly shocking to Allen, who preferred the gospel straight, was a decision which authorized the wearing of gowns and robes by preachers. "... I have thought," Allen wrote in a typically dry and sardonic utterance, "that religion has been declining in the church ever since."

Within two years, Allen found himself in the middle of a controversy that went to the heart of the meaning of the church. The surface issue revolved around the place of black people in the church. But this issue was linked to the deeper, more ominous question of the place of free black people in American life.

In February, 1786, when Richard Allen returned to Philadelphia for a visit, black and white Americans were groping toward a new relationship. Philadelphia at the time was the largest and most important American city. As the temporary national capital and a center of liberal Quaker influence, the city was a magnet for black people who received their freedom in the Revolutionary War.

In the 1780's, the black population increased enormously. So did fear, guilt, and anxiety. The core problem was the bitter antagonism between poor whites and free black people. Above all else, poor whites resented and feared the economic threat of a colony of hungry and desperately poor freedmen. The resentment and fear exerted a subtle influence on all institutions, including the church, which began to draw invidious distinctions between black and white parishioners. Richard Allen, watching the drift of the age, concluded that the day of white Christians bathing the feet of black Christians was gone forever. And he put his finger on another fact: a radical alteration in the mood of black men. There was a new spirit of self-assertion abroad. Black men were no longer willing to accept gratuitous slurs and deprecations. Perceiving this, Allen decided to tarry awhile in Philadelphia. He wrote: "I soon saw a large field in seeking and instructing my African brethren, who had been a long forgotten people, and few of them attended public worship."

Allen did not have to wait long. When the black Christians were pulled from their knees at St. George's, the black community of Philadelphia mobilized for action. Under the leadership of Allen, and Absalom Jones, free black men formed a pioneer black organization, the Free African Society of Philadelphia, which W. E. B. Du Bois called "the first wavering step of a people toward organized group life." The society, which was formed on April 12, 1787, was a non-sectarian religious organization. But it also functioned as a mutual aid society. The society's mutual aid department marked the beginning of a major black business, the insurance company. Similar societies were formed in Boston, Providence, Rhode Island, and other cities and served as a link between the free black colonies of the North.

Out of the Free African Society came two pioneer church groups: the Free African Church of St. Thomas (Episcopal) with Absalom Jones as rector, and Bethel African Methodist

Episcopal Church with Richard Allen as guiding light. After twenty-two years of conflict and litigation, Bethel became in 1816 an independent church. In this same year, sixteen Methodist leaders from independent church groups convened and formed a national organization, the African Methodist Episcopal Church. Allen, interestingly enough, was not chosen the first bishop. This honor went to Daniel Coker, an eloquent Baltimore preacher who was elected bishop on April 9, 1816, the first day of the conference. According to tradition, the light-skinned Coker, the son of a slave and a white woman, was too fair for some of the delegates. Coker was persuaded to resign and Richard Allen was elected bishop the next day. Allen was then fifty-six and at the height of his considerable powers.

A blunt-speaking, strong-willed man, with brown skin of "a soft chestnut tint" and piercing eyes, Allen threw himself into the work of developing the collective will of the black people. As a preacher and bishop, he made his church a strong force in Afro-American life. But he also contributed substantially in the fields of protest and improvement. A longtime believer in education, he founded a night school for adults and a day school for children. He also told his flock not to take literally the biblical injunction against laying up treasures on earth. Allen, incidentally, was independently wealthy, with a thriving boot and shoe store and large real estate holdings.

The whole range of black life came under the eye and hand of the black bishop. In most civic ventures, he was paired with his friend, Absalom Jones. Although the two men differed on doctrinal matters, they were united in all things pertaining to racial progress. Jones is virtually unknown today, but he held a high place in the hearts of his contemporaries. Easygoing and mild-mannered, the Episcopal rector was a perfect foil for the blunt Allen, who was fourteen years his junior. Together, the two men walked the streets of Philadelphia, prodding their people and rousing them for defense and attack.

Allen and Jones were among the outstanding heroes of the Philadelphia yellow fever epidemics of 1792-93. Black emergency units, under their direction, nursed victims and disposed of bodies. When a white author criticized the contributions of the black emergency units, Allen and Jones penned an eloquent defense in a pamphlet which also attacked slavery and prejudice. The two men argued that the social characteristics of black people were a direct result of enforced degradation and tyranny. They warned of the perils of slavery and added: "If you love your children, if you love your country, if you love the God of love, clear your hands from slaves, burden not your children or your country with them." Allen and Jones concluded with a poem which reminded Americans of the war services of black people.

> *God and a soldier all men do adore*
> *In time of war and not before;*
> *When the war is over, and all things righted,*
> *God is forgotten, and the soldier slighted.*

Throughout this period, Allen and Jones hammered at the conscience of America. They were aided by another outstanding Philadelphia leader, James Forten. Forten was a Revolutionary War veteran and wealthy manufacturer who amassed a $100,000 fortune and employed both black and white artisans in his sail factory.

The Philadelphia trio—Allen, Jones, and Forten—circulated petitions and devised new methods for attacking discrimination and segregation. Jones was the leader of a group of Philadelphians who sent an antislavery petition to Congress in 1800. Forten attracted national attention with a series of letters which demolished the arguments of whites who wanted to limit the freedom of movement for free black people.

During the first two decades of the nineteenth century, Allen, Jones, and Forten focused their fire on the rising colonization movement. After the unsuccessful Gabriel Prosser conspiracy in Virginia and the successful Toussaint Louverture revolution in Haiti, white men began to legislate for their lives. Numerous proposals were advanced for the deportation, voluntary and involuntary, of free Negroes, who were considered social pariahs and a dangerous influence on slaves. This agitation reached a peak in 1816 with the formation of the American Colonization Society. To the dismay of Allen and other black people, the colonizationists picked up considerable official support in Washington. Congress finally appropriated money which was used to establish Liberia. On February 6, 1820, the "Friendship"—"the Mayflower of Liberia"—departed from New York City with eighty-six Afro-Americans.

Colonization was not an entirely new issue to the Philadelphians. The Negro Union of Newport, Rhode Island, had suggested an exodus of free Afro-Americans in 1788. The Philadelphia Society, under the leadership of Allen and Jones, had replied: "With regard to the emigration to Africa you mention we have at present but little to communicate on that head, apprehending every pious man is a good citizen of the whole world."

This viewpoint was not shared by all Afro-Americans. Some, despairing of the good faith and the good sense of white Americans, championed a return to Africa. Allen's chief rival, Daniel Coker, and John B. Russwurm, the first black college graduate, were among the first converts to the colonization cause. But the vast majority of free men held fast, contending that they were Americans—African-Americans—and that their first duty was to their brothers in bondage. Black leaders charged that colonizationists were generally anti-Negro and pro-slavery. "The colonizationists," one black man said, "want us to go to Liberia if we will. If we won't go there, we may go to hell."

Thoroughly alarmed by the climate of repression stimulated by the colonization controversy, free Afro-Americans counterattacked. For the first time in America, they utilized mass pressure techniques. Mass meetings were organized in Richmond, New York, and Boston. Richard Allen, Absalom Jones, and James Forten organized a pioneer mass meeting which met in Bethel Church in January, 1817. Forten was chairman of the meeting which declared that free Negroes would never abandon the slaves who are "our brethren by the ties of consanguinity, of suffering, and of wrong." The mass meeting named a committee of eleven, including Allen, Jones, and Forten, to correspond with the Philadelphia congressmen. Allen later wrote an anticolonization article for the first black newspaper, *Freedom's Journal.*

An indirect result of the colonization controversy was a closely knit national black group with a common viewpoint and a consciousness of a common fate. Richard Allen watched this development with mixed emotions. He believed with all his heart in the oneness of man. But he also believed that black people had to unite before they could integrate.

Events in the 1820's did nothing to controvert his point of view. The Age of Jackson and the Common (white) Man ushered in a period of extreme reaction for black people. Antagonism between white workers and free black men reached new heights, and municipal bodies received a flurry of anti-black petitions. Some petitioners argued for the forcible expulsion of free Negroes. Others called for additional laws to protect the livelihood and psychological security of white workers. More ominous was the wave of riots which began in Cincinnati in 1827 and leaped across the North.

From his house on Spruce Street, Allen measured the force of the gathering storm. He was an old man now and his life was drawing to a close. He could look back on a life full of toil and achievement. He was worth upwards of forty thousand dollars and his family was secure. His six children—four boys and two girls—were provided for. The church was established and his young assistant, Bishop Morris Brown, was feeding the faithful. There were friends, memories, and the companionship of a devoted wife, Sarah. And yet Allen was not satisfied. Nearing seventy and the grave, he roused himself for one last effort on behalf of his people.

On his desk was a letter from Hezekiah Grice, a young man from Baltimore who proposed a national Negro convention. As the tide of oppression rolled over the North, Allen decided that the time had come to hold a convention. Circulars were written and important leaders were contacted. On the appointed day, Grice arrived in Philadelphia with eyes bright in anticipation. Approaching a black man on the street, he inquired about the response to the convention. The man replied testily, "Who ever heard of colored people holding a convention—convention, indeed!"

Crestfallen, Grice made his way to Bethel Church, where he found five men "in solemn conclave." Finally, on September 20, 1830, the first black convention in American history opened with forty delegates from Pennsylvania, Rhode Island, Virginia, New York, Maryland, Delaware, and Connecticut. The group elected Richard Allen president and proceeded to discuss the state of the race. The resolutions recommended united action against the forces of hate and ill-will and condemned the American Colonization Society. A second convention was authorized for the following year.

Richard Allen was not destined to chair the second convention. He died on March 26, 1831. A contemporary newspaper reported: "The immense concourse of coloured people, who attended the funeral of this pious patriarch, exceeded perhaps anything of its kind ever witnessed in this country. No other African corpse, it is presumed, was ever attended to the place of interment, in America, by as great a number, or more sincere mourners."

Allen spent his last years in the shadow of a new breed of

black leaders. Most of these men were more militant than Allen. Yet almost all of them hailed Allen, Forten, Jones, Varick, and other pioneers who ran the first leg of the black man's odyssey in America. Perhaps the best tribute came from David Walker, who also wrote the most radical antislavery pamphlet.

"Richard Allen, O my God!" Walker wrote. "The bare recollection of the labors of this man and his ministrations among his deplorably wretched brethren (rendered so by the whites) to bring them to a knowledge of the God of Heaven, fills my soul with all those high emotions which would take the pen of Addison to portray. It is impossible, my brethren, for me to say much in this work respecting that man of God. When the Lord shall raise up coloured historians in succeeding generations, to present the crimes of this nation to the then gazing world, the Holy Ghost will make them do justice to the name of Richard Allen of Philadelphia."

FOUNDERS
of the
BLACK PRESS

———◆———

Samuel E. Cornish
and
John B. Russwurm

We wish to plead our own cause.

OPENING EDITORIAL,
FREEDOM'S JOURNAL, 1827

SAMUEL E. CORNISH   *JOHN B. RUSSWURM*

DAY IN AND day out, the black people of New York City were mercilessly lampooned in the white press. In the dying days of 1826, the campaign of vilification and slander reached nauseous heights. The integrity and courage of black men were openly questioned. Worse, editors invaded homes and impugned the chastity of black women.

The leader of this campaign was Mordecai M. Noah, an eccentric dramatist and entrepreneur who controlled several newspapers at various times. Obsessed by what he considered black degradation, he pushed a bitterly personal one man crusade. And his crusade was the proximate or immediate cause of the founding of what became the largest and most powerful minority press in America. For it was to devise a defense against the scurrilous attacks of this editor that New York leaders came together in the early weeks of 1827. Meeting in the home of Boston Crummell, the patriarch of the black community, the leaders decided that black people could not depend on either their friends or their enemies for a complete articulation of their ideals and aspirations. After a long and heated discussion, the black leaders decided to organize a newspaper to answer not only the charges of individual editors, but also the collective assault of white America on the black psyche.

This was a time of acute crisis for all Afro-Americans and the New York leaders were agonizingly conscious of the forces arrayed against them. Bread was dear in every ghetto, and anti-Negro riots were common. More ominous was the creeping power of the American Colonization Society. Not only the Negro's enemies, notably the New York editor, but also his friends, notably Benjamin Lundy, Gerrit Smith, and, before 1830, William Lloyd Garrison, were saying that Negroes would probably be better off in a hotter climate — Africa, one wit put it, or either hell.

Samuel E. Cornish and John B. Russwurm, two of the youngest and most promising of the New York leaders, were assigned the task of inventing a journal that could speak forcibly to both the enemy and faint friend without and the "brethren" within, the veil. Cornish and Russwurm were eminently fitted for the task. Both were of free stock, and both were articulate exponents of persistent protest. Cornish, who is virtually unknown today, was born about 1795 in Delaware and raised in the relatively free environments of Philadelphia and New York City. After graduating from the Free African schools, he became a minister and organized the first black Presbyterian Church on New Demeter Street in Manhattan.

Russwurm, who is generally credited with being the first black graduate of an American college, was a Jamaican, the son of a white man and a Negro woman. His father, motivated perhaps by a sense of guilt, sent him secretly to a Canadian school where he was registered under the name of John Brown. The father neglected to inform his white wife of the sins of his youth; but after his death, the widow learned of the existence of the son and insisted that "John Brown" assume his rightful name of John B. Russwurm. She also financed Russwurm's education at Bowdoin, where he was graduated in 1826.

Despite the difference in their backgrounds, Russwurm and Cornish made an excellent team. Cornish, the idealist and uncompromising fighter, complemented Russwurm, who was a pragmatist dedicated to "the art of the possible."

Samuel E. Cornish and John B. Russwurm

With the idealistic Cornish at the helm as senior editor and the practical Russwurm in second place as junior editor, the black-owned and black-operated publishing company confounded the skeptics by making tangible steps toward what many considered an impossible goal, the publishing of a black newspaper. The prospectus for the proposed paper was a masterly blend of idealism and practicality. "We shall ever regard the constitution of the United States as our polar star," Cornish and Russwurm wrote. "Pledged to no party, we shall endeavor to urge our brethren to use their rights to the elective franchise as free citizens. It shall never be our object to court controversy though we must at all times consider ourselves as champions in defense of oppressed humanity. Daily slandered, we think that there ought to be some channel of communication between us and the public, through which a single voice may be heard, in defense of five hundred thousand free people of colour. Too often has injustice been heaped upon us, when our only defense was an appeal to the Almighty, but we believe that the time has now arrived, when the calumnies of our enemies should be refuted by forcible arguments. . . ."

On Friday, March 16, 1827, the first issue of *Freedom's Journal*, the first black newspaper in the Western world, appeared on the streets of New York City. In the first editorial, Cornish and Russwurm struck a note that is as modern as today's headlines.

We wish to plead our own cause. Too long have others spoken for us. Too long has the publick been deceived by misrepresentations, in things which concern us dearly, though in the estimation of some mere trifles; for though there are many in society who exercise towards us benevolent feelings; still (with sorrow we confess it) there are others who make it their business to enlarge upon the least trifle, which tends to the discredit of any person of colour! and pronounce anathemas and denounce our whole body for the misconduct of this guilty one. . . .

Our vices and our degradation are ever arrayed against us, but our virtues are passed by unnoticed. And what is still more lamentable, our friends, to whom we concede all the principles of humanity and religion, from these very causes seem to have fallen into the current of popular feeling and are imperceptibly floating on the stream—actually living in the practice of prejudice, while they abjure it in theory, and feel it not in their hearts. Is it not very desirable that such should know more of our actual conditions; and of our efforts and feelings, that in forming or advocating plans for our amelioration, they may do it more understandingly?

Having stated succinctly the immediate causes of the founding of the black press—the calumnies of enemies and the timidity of avowed friends—Cornish and Russwurm went on to take their stands on the great rocks of the black press—civil rights in general and the ballot in particular. "The civil rights of a people being of the greatest value, it shall ever be our duty to vindicate our brethren, when oppressed; and to lay the case before the publick. We shall also urge upon our brethren ... the expediency of using their elective franchise; and of making an independent use of the same. We wish them not to become the tools of the party."

As for policy, the editors pledged themselves to print "everything that relates to Africa" and to hold up always the banner of the downtrodden, especially the slaves "[who] are our kindred by all the ties of nature."

"It is our earnest wish," the first editorial of the first black newspaper said, "to make our Journal a medium of intercourse between our brethren in the different states of this great confederacy; that through its columns an expression of our sentiments, on many interesting subjects which concern us, may be offered to the publick; that plans which apparently are beneficial may be candidly discussed and properly weighed; if worthy, receive our cordial approbation; if not, our marked disapprobation."

In these historic words, Cornish and Russwurm stated the mission and purpose of the black press which some students believe to be the most powerful institution in the black community. Indeed, Myrdal and others have asserted that the Negro press created the Afro-American as a social and political being.

Back there, 141 years ago, only a few men recognized the power and potential of the paper with the prophetic title, *Freedom's Journal.* The paper, in truth, was a modest thing. In structure and conception, it was more a magazine than a newspaper. Not more than two of the sixteen columns were devoted to foreign and domestic news. The remaining columns were filled with material not unlike the stories and features in *Ebony* and other black-oriented magazines. The first issue, for example, contained the first installment of the "Memoirs" of Paul Cuffee, the black captain, a report on the illegal imprisonment of a poet, articles on the "Common Schools of New York," and "The Church and the Auction Block," "A True Story," an essay on "The Effect of Sight Upon a Person Born Blind," antislavery material, entertainment and variety departments. There was even an article with disguised sex appeal, "On Choosing a Wife By Proxy." Also included in the paper were notices of marriages, deaths, and court trials. Commercial advertisements were printed on the last page.

The paper was published every Friday at No. 5 Varick Street in Manhattan. Free Afro-Americans in all sections of the country, and in Canada, Haiti, and England, rallied to the support of the *Journal*, organizing local societies. Among the prominent Afro-Americans who served as correspondents were James Forten, David Walker, and Richard Allen.

Like John H. Johnson of *Ebony, Jet*, and *Negro Digest*, like John Sengstacke of the *Chicago Defender* and Carl Murphy of the *Afro-American*, Cornish and Russwurm stressed those facets of the Afro-American personality which are ignored in white media. Negro achievement, as expressed in the careers of Phillis Wheatley, Toussaint Louverture, and Richard Allen, was prominently featured in *Freedom's Journal*. Race pride, another value of the modern black press, was also emphasized.

Freedom's Journal played an extremely important role not only as a protest journal, but also as an instrument for revealing the human dimension of the Afro-American personality. White men of that day scoffed at the idea of love and family ties among Afro-Americans. By featuring the Afro-American as a parent, a bride, a mother or a father, the paper exposed the one-dimensional treatment of the Afro-American in the white press.

Since the paper was founded, at least in part, as a reaction to the slurs on black women, Cornish and Russwurm played up the trials and triumphs of black mothers and wives, noting:

> *Black I am, oh daughter fair*
> *But my beauty is most rare.*

Cornish and Russwurm were black editors, but they were also editors who published a great deal of literary and scientific material which had no immediate bearing on race. "Only a strong necessity," they said, forced them to stress race. And it would be necessary, they said, to stress race as long as the "strong necessity" existed, as long, in fact, as the white press refused to present black people in the totality of their being.

As shapers and reflectors of Afro-American opinion and sentiment, the two pioneer editors prepared public opinion for the antislavery crusade. Long before William Lloyd Garrison, they advocated immediate emancipation and unconditional freedom with full civil rights. In fact, *Freedom's Journal* and Samuel E. Cornish were largely responsible for the conversion of the early white abolitionists, who were, as one leader put it, being "swept away by the waves of expatriation."

For two years, *Freedom's Journal* served as a beacon for both black and white protestants. Cornish retained an interest in the *Journal* throughout this period, but he resigned the senior editorship in September, 1827, and became an agent for the Free African schools. Russwurm succeeded him as editor. But Russwurm, as it turned out, was undergoing a crisis of conscience. As the flames of fear and phobia leaped higher and higher, Russwurm became convinced that the American Colonization

Society was right. In February, 1829, he announced his support of "the return to Africa movement." Enraged black leaders forced him to resign and accused him of "selling out" to the enemies of black people. Russwurm maintained that he was sincere; but this was no comfort to black leaders, who burned him in effigy.

By this time, Russwurm had moved to a position that would be called black nationalism today. Believing that the "man of color would never find a place in the Western Hemisphere to lay his head," he called for a return to Africa and a revival of the great empires of the Middle Ages. What angered other black leaders was his acceptance of a liberal offer from the conservative Maryland Colonization Society and his defense of the black exclusion laws of Ohio because "our rightful place is in Africa."

After receiving an M.A. degree from Bowdoin College in 1829, Russwurm sailed for Liberia, where he founded the *Liberia Herald* and served as superintendent of schools. He later became famous as governor of the Maryland Colony at Cape Palmas. The pioneer editor died in Liberia in 1851.

Black leaders of the nineteenth century never forgave Russwurm for his alleged defection. Until the latter part of the century, they were almost unanimous in deprecation of Russwurm and praise of Cornish. Today, in one of history's strange little jests, Russwurm is universally praised and Cornish is forgotten.

After Russwurm's forced resignation, Cornish resumed editorial control of *Freedom's Journal*. In May, 1829, two months after the temporary suspension of the *Journal*, Cornish started a new paper, *The Rights of All*. Thereafter, he was associated with a number of periodicals. He was also a member of the executive committee of the board of the American Antislavery Society and was probably the first black American to champion Tuskegee-type trade schools.

Cornish, unlike Russwurm, called for a fight to the finish in America. "Let there be no compromise," he said, "but as though born free and equal, let us contend for all the rights guaranteed by the constitution of our native country."

As for the designation "American," Cornish contended that black people had a better right to the word than most white men. "Many," he said, "would rob us of the endeared name, 'American,' a description more emphatically belonging to us, than to five-sixths of this nation, and one that we will never yield."

Cornish's lonely and uncompromising fight nerved weaker men. And he was, in part, responsible for the survival of the black press as an effective instrument of protest. Before the Civil War, some twenty-four newspapers sprang up to champion the cause of men Cornish called "Colored Americans." During this same period, the pioneer black magazines appeared: the *National Reformer* in 1833, the *Mirror of Liberty* in 1837, and the *African Methodist Episcopal Review* in 1841.

Men made in the image of Cornish and other pioneers of the black press carried the fight into the enemy camp and validated the black man's right to soil fertilized by the blood and tears of black men and women. By 1841, it was clear to almost everyone that the Afro-American was here to stay and that room would have to be made for him.

Today, more than a century after the founding of *Freedom's Journal*, the same message leaps from the pages of hundreds of newspapers and magazines that are lengthened shadows of Cornish and Russwurm who, as Bella Gross said, delivered "the first authentic messages of the New Negro to the World."

THE FANON
of the
NINETEENTH CENTURY

———◆———

David Walker

> What a happy country this will be, if the
> whites will listen....But Americans, I
> declare to you, while you keep us and our
> children in bondage, and treat us like brutes,
> to make us support you and your families,
> . we cannot be your friends.
>
> DAVID WALKER

HE WAS A FIREBELL which wouldn't stop ringing.
He came out of the South, vibrating with the indignities of slavery, and he rang with such force and clarity that some men couldn't rest until the bell of his life had been stilled.

His name was David Walker. He was a free black man. His mission was the liberation of the colored peoples of the world — by whatever means necessary.

Walker's theater of action was the printed page. He was a propagandist, a theorist, a man of words. But words to Walker were acts, not ways of avoiding acts. And he used words to act upon slavery and the supporters of slavery.

Nothing indicates this more strikingly than the main act of his life, the publication, in 1829, of a slim, seventy-six-page book with the imposing title: *David Walker's Appeal To The COLOURED CITIZENS OF THE WORLD, but in particular and very expressly, to those of THE UNITED STATES OF AMERICA.* In this work, which caused consternation in white America, Walker sounded the doom of the slave system and told the slaves it was their Christian duty to slit their oppressors' throats from ear to ear. "O Americans! Americans!!!" he wrote. "I call God — I call angels — I call men, to witness, that your *DESTRUCTION is at hand*, and will be *speedily consummated unless you REPENT.*" So writing and so believing, Walker anticipated the twentieth century's Frantz Fanon and inaugurated the militant movement for black liberation in America.

The appearance of David Walker marked a transition in the liberation movement from the quiet protest of the colonial leaders to the revolutionary posture of the militant abolitionists. Even more importantly, Walker recalled and refocused the militant tradition of direct and open defiance which characterized the first generation of Afro-Americans.

It was this tradition, flowing out of the ethos of Africa, which animated the black colonial rebels who stood toe to toe with the colonial slavemasters, hacking, maiming, and burning. It was this tradition which prompted a lieutenant governor of Virginia in 1730 to order white men to take their pistols to church with them. It was this tradition and the fear that it spawned that seared the spirit of America and made the slave South a prison.

When, in 1785, David Walker was born, the tradition of defiance was still a burning presence in the breasts of the slaves. Fifteen years after his birth, Gabriel Prosser led an unsuccessful slave revolt in Virginia. Twenty-two years later, Denmark Vesey planned and almost executed a revolutionary uprising in Charleston, South Carolina.

David Walker came to maturity within the compass of these events. He was born free on September 28, 1785, in Wilmington, North Carolina. His father, a slave, died before he was born; and he was raised by his mother, a free black woman. He apparently learned to read and write. He tells us in his book that he traveled widely and that he loathed oppression. So embittered was he by the barbarism of slavery that he resolved to seek a freer climate.

"If I remain in this bloody land," he told himself, "I will not live long. As true as God reigns, I will be avenged for the sorrow which my people have suffered. This is not the place for me—no, no. I must leave this part of the country. It will be a great trial for me to live on the same soil where so many men are in slavery; certainly I cannot remain where I must hear their chains continually, and where I must encounter the insults of their hypocritical enslavers. Go, I must."

And so, feeling thus, Walker went, settling some time in the 1820's in Boston, where he applied himself with diligence to study and work. For some four years, a contemporary said, he was "hurtfully indefatigable" in his studies. He was also active in the economic field, accumulating enough money to open a second-hand clothing store on Brattle Street near the docks. But it quickly became apparent that Walker's business was revolution, not business. During and after business hours, he shuttled from group to group, preaching solidarity and manly assertion. He also plugged into the currents of the developing national movement by serving as Boston correspondent of *Freedom's Journal.*

As a writer and speaker, Walker became known for his revolutionary tone and his radical appraisals. Then and later, he railed against the artificial distinctions within the black group and urged support of black leaders and black institutions. He was vocal on the virtues of revolutionary education. It was the duty of every black man, he said, to disseminate education and truth. Speaking to the free black elite of his day, he said: "I call upon you therefore to cast your eyes upon the wretchedness of your brethren, and to do your utmost to enlighten them —go to work and enlighten your brethren!"

Walker practiced what he preached. Wherever he went, he raised inconvenient questions and pointed to the hard road of duty. "I promiscuously fell in conversation once," he later wrote, "with an elderly coloured man on the topics of education, and of the great prevalency of ignorance among us: Said he, 'I know that our people are very ignorant, but my son has a good education: I spent a great deal of money on his education: He can write as well as any man, and I assure you that no one can fool him...'" Walker questioned the man closely and brought out that the son's education had little relevance to his needs and the needs of his people. Walker heaped scorn on that kind of education and said: "I pray that the Lord may undeceive my ignorant brethren, and permit them to throw away pretensions, and seek after the substance of learning." As for himself, Walker said: "I would crawl on my hands and knees through mud and mire, to the feet of a learned man, where I would sit and humbly supplicate him to instill into me, that which neither devils nor tyrants could remove, only with my life — for coloured people to acquire learning in this country, makes tyrants quake and tremble on their sandy foundation." An educated man, in Walker's view, was a revolutionary man, particularly in a situation of oppression. "Do you suppose," he asked, "that one man of good sense and learning would submit himself, his father, mother, wife and children, to be slaves to a wretched man like himself, who, instead of compensating him for his labours, chains, hand-cuffs and beats him and his family almost to death, leaving life enough in them, however, to work for, and call him master. No! No! he would cut his devilish throat from ear to ear, and well do slave-holders know it. The bare name of educating the coloured people, scares our cruel oppressors almost to death..."

On another occasion, Walker met a black man with a string of boots on his shoulders. "We fell into conversation," Walker reported, "and in the course of which, I said to him, what a miserable set of people we are! He asked, why? — Said I, we are so subjected under the whites, that we cannot obtain the comforts of life, but by cleaning their boots and shoes, selling old clothes, waiting on them, shaving them. Said he, (with the boots on his shoulders) 'I am completely happy!!! I never want to live any better or happier than when I can get plenty of boots and shoes to clean!!!' Oh! How can those who are actuated by avarice only, but think, that our Creator made us to be an inheritance to them forever, when they see that our greatest glory is centered in such mean and low objects? Understand me, brethren, I do not mean to speak against the occupations by which we acquire enough and sometimes scarcely that, to render ourselves and families comfortable through life. I am subjected to the same inconvenience, as you all. —My objections are, to our *glorying* and being *happy* in such low employments; for if we are men, we ought to be thankful to the Lord for the past, and for the future."

Walker was scornful of the efforts of black and white colonizationists who wanted to return Afro-Americans to Africa. "America," he said, "is more our country, than it is the whites — we have enriched it with our blood and tears. The greatest riches in all America have arisen from our blood and tears: —and will they drive us from our property and homes, which we have earned with our blood? They must look sharp or this very thing will bring swift destruction upon them."

Thus David Walker, a teacher without a classroom, a revolutionary in search of a cadre, a man obsessed, always agitating, always pointing, always *signifying*.

As Walker moved among his contemporaries, studying their condition and their aspirations, instructing and scolding, he conceived the idea of confronting the future with a book. By the middle of 1827, this idea had become the all-consuming passion of his life, blotting out all other considerations. One can imagine him in this period walking dazedly through the narrow Boston streets. One can picture him in his rooms, summoning words of horror. He tells us that he wrote the book in a passion of indignation "with eyes streaming with tears," and with his ears ringing "with the cries, tears and groans of his oppressed people."

Walker's book startled.

It was, in fact, more than a book — it was an event, a *happening*.

Men who saw it in that light were not deceived. For, Fanon apart, there has never been another book quite like it in the history of black-white relations in America.

First of all and most importantly of all, Walker's *Appeal* was addressed to the revolutionary consciousness of the oppressed, not to the Christian conscience of the oppressor. Like Fanon, more than a hundred years later, Walker bypassed the missionary and the do-gooder and spoke directly to the disinherited. And he spoke in tones of revolutionary indignation. In his imagery, in his rhetoric, Walker made clear what he was about. He was not writing another Christian appeal to white men; he was writing a revolutionary manual for the black men of the world; for it was, he said, an "unshaken and for ever immovable *fact,* that your full glory and happiness as well as all other coloured people under Heaven, shall never be fully consummated, but with the *entire emancipation of your enslaved brethren all over the world.*"

Camus said once that the only philosophical question is the question of suicide. Concerning which, one might reply that, for the oppressed, the only philosophical question is homicide.

Walker confronted that question. More than any other American writer, before or afterwards, Walker grappled with the question of violence. And he began his disquisition by charging that oppression was in and of itself violence. Therefore, the question of the counterviolence of the oppressed was at best academic and at worst mystification. In a situation maintained by the violence of the oppressor, the only solution, he said, was violence by the oppressed. More than one hundred years before Fanon, Walker said that violence was cathartic and necessary for the oppressed. Unlike Sorel and Engels, Walker did not offer a long theoretical argument in defense of counterviolence. To him, it was self-evident. It was as natural, he said, as taking a drink of water. "Now," he wrote, "I ask you, had you not rather be killed than to be a slave to a tyrant, who takes the life of your mother, wife, and dear little children, and answer God Almighty: and believe this, that it is no more harm for you to kill a man, who is trying to kill you, than it is for you to take a drink of water when thirsty; in fact, the man who will stand still and let another murder him, is worse than infidel, and, if he has common sense, ought not to be pitied."

Walker did not pity the oppressed; he prodded them, saying it was their Christian duty to rise up and wage a war to the knife on the enemies of man.

Walker reached this melancholy conclusion by a rigorous examination of the obstacles and the options. He asked himself, first of all, the cause of the wretchedness of his people. And he answered: slavery. And what was the cause of slavery? Greed, Walker answered—that and the historic miscarriage of white European civilization.

Although Walker wrote out of a religious framework, he identified the primary problem as economic exploitation. White people, he said, were determined to live out of the blood and sweat of black people. They wanted black people "to dig their mines and work their farms; and thus go on enriching them, from one generation to another with our *blood* and our *tears*!!!" Some whites were so corrupted by greed for gold that they believed, Walker charged, that God made them "to sit in the shade, and make the blacks work without remuneration for their services." As a matter of fact, Walker added, "the labour of slaves comes so cheap to the avaricious usurpers, and is (as they think) of such great utility to the countries where it exists, that those who are actuated by sordid avarice only, overlook the evils, which will sure as the Lord lives, follow after the good."

In Walker's view, Euro-Americans had corrupted themselves —perhaps beyond redemption. "The whites," he wrote, "have always been an unjust, jealous, unmerciful, avaricious and blood-thirsty set of beings, always seeking after power and authority. —We view them all over the confederacy of Greece, where they were first known to be anything, (in consequence of education) we see them there, cutting each other's throats—trying to subject each other to wretchedness and misery—to effect which, they used all kinds of deceitful, unfair, and unmerciful means. We view them next in Rome, where the spirit of tyranny and deceit raged still higher. We view them in Gaul, Spain, and in Britain. —In fine, we view them all over Europe, together with what were scattered about in Asia and Africa, as heathens, and we see them acting more like devils than accountable men. But some may ask, did not the blacks of Africa, and the mulattoes of Asia, go on in the same way as did the whites of Europe. I answer, no—they never were half so avaricious, deceitful and unmerciful as the whites, according to their knowledge." Walker said that the conversion of the Europeans to Christianity had not improved their morals. "In fact, take them as a body, they are ten times more cruel, avaricious and unmerciful than ever they were." Walker went on to question whether whites were "as good by nature" as the blacks and he suggested "that if ever the world becomes Christianized, (which must certainly take place before long) it will be through the means, under God, of the Blacks."

Walker said white people had made themselves "the natural enemies" of black people. "I say, "Walker wrote, "from the beginning, I do not think that we were natural enemies to each other. But the whites having made us so wretched, by subjecting us to slavery, and having murdered so many millions of us, in order to make us work for them, and out of devilishness— and they taking our wives, whom we love as we do ourselves— our mothers, who bore the pains of death to give us birth—our fathers and dear little children, and ourselves, and strip and beat us one before the other—chain, hand-cuff, and drag us about like rattlesnakes—shoot us down like wild bears, before each other's faces, to make us submissive to, and work to support them and their families.... They (the whites) know well, if we are *men* ... and see them treating us in the manner they do, that there can be nothing in our hearts but death alone, for them ... Man, in all ages and all nations of the earth, is the same...."

White oppression, Walker said, had had an unfortunate effect on Afro-Americans who were ignorant, divided and permeated by a mean and servile spirit. Like Fanon, Walker hid nothing. Like Fanon, he was pitiless in his exposure of the weaknesses of the colonized. He saw black men "grovelling in submission," "protecting devils and fighting each other." All of this, he said, was a result of ignorance which he called "the mother of treachery and deceit." In a prophetic insight, he charged that ignorance was not only the product of oppression but the aim and the intent of the system of oppression. White people, he said, were promoting ignorance in the black population. Worse, missionaries and "preachers of Jesus Christ" were conditioning the blacks to a state of servility by a pervasive campaign of brainwashing. "O! save us, we pray thee, thou God of Heaven and of earth, from the devouring hands of the white Christians!!!"

Reviewing this catalogue of social evils, Walker was overcome ("Oh Heaven! I am full!!! I can hardly move my pen!!!") by a thirst for vengeance and he asked: "Can the Americans escape God Almighty?" He said he hoped white people would see the errors of their ways and repent, but he was not hopeful. At any rate, he said, some whites were beyond the pale of redemption.

A curse, he said, hung over the land. The cup of America was "nearly full." The day was "fast approaching, when (unless there is a universal repentance on the part of the whites, which will scarcely take place, they have got to be so hardened in consequence of our blood, and so wise in their own conceit.)" White people, moreover, had degraded black people and taught them "the art of throat-cutting." And "some of them," he said, "would curse the day they ever saw us."

Walker issued a clarion call for black men to stand up like men and stop submitting—whatever the cost. "I ask you, oh my brethren!" he wrote, "are we MEN? Did our Creator make us to be slaves to dust and ashes like ourselves? Are they not dying worms as well as we?" And he added: "If ever we become men (I mean respectable men, such as other people are) we must exert ourselves to the full. . . ."

What did this mean?

It meant, Walker said, a holy war against the usurpers.

Walker commended black men to the care of "the God of the armies," the God of Abraham and Jacob and Isaac. *That* God, Walker said, "will give you a Hannibal." He urged black men to *watch* for ". . . the day of our redemption from the abject wretchedness draweth near, when we shall be enabled, in the most extended sense of the word, to stretch forth our hands to the LORD our God, but there must be a willingness on our part, for God to do these things for us, for we may be assured that he will not take us by the hairs of our head against our will and desire, and drag us from our very mean, low and abject condition." Black people, he said, had been misrepresented. There "is an unconquerable disposition in the breasts of the blacks, which, when it is fully awakened and put in motion, will be subdued, only with the destruction of the animal existence. Get the blacks started, and if you do not have a gang of tigers and lions to deal with, I am a deceiver of the blacks and of the whites."

Walker was horrified by the destruction he foresaw. "But," he said, "when I reflect that God is just, and that millions of my wretched brethren would meet death with glory, yea, more, would plunge into the very mouths of cannons and be torn into particles as minute as the atoms which compose the elements of the earth, in preference to a mean submission to the lash of tyrants, I am with streaming eyes, compelled to shrink back into nothingness before my Maker, and exclaim again, thy will be done, O Lord God Almighty."

The harvest was at hand, and Walker called for strong and

steady laborers. He recommended careful planning and deliberate action. "Never make an attempt to gain our freedom or *natural right*," he said, "from under our cruel oppressors and murderers, until you see your way clear—when that hour arrives and you move, be not afraid or dismayed; for be you assured that Jesus Christ the King of heaven and of earth who is the God of justice and of armies, will surely go before you." He added: "... if you commence, make sure work—do not trifle, for they will not trifle with you—they want us for their slaves, and think nothing of murdering us in order to subject us to that wretched condition—therefore, if there is an *attempt* made by us, kill or be killed."

There was no need, Walker said, for fear or doubt. "Can our condition be any worse?" he asked. "If there are any changes, will they not be for the better, though they may appear for the worse at first? Can they get us any lower? Where can they get us? They are afraid to treat us worse, for they know well, the day they do it they are gone."

Walker concluded with a solemn word of warning to Americans. "I speak, Americans," he said, "for your good. We must and shall be free I say, in spite of you. You may do your best to keep us in wretchedness and misery, to enrich you and your children; but God will deliver us from under you. And woe, woe will be to you if we have to obtain our freedom by fighting."

Walker flung his completed book like a spear at the hearts of his contemporaries and they fled precipitately from the sharp tips of his words. Within a year, the book went through three editions and copies turned up in several Southern states. White abolitionists like William Lloyd Garrison and Benjamin Lundy immediately disowned the book, deprecating its violent tone. Said Lundy: "A more bold, daring, inflammatory publication, perhaps, never issued from the press of any country. I can do no less than set the broadest seal of condemnation on it. Such things have no earthly effect than to injure our cause."

In the South, the reviews were more hysterical. The *Greensborough Patriot* said: "If Perkins' steam-gun had been charged with rattle-snakes, and shot into the midst of a flock of wild pigeons, the fluttering could not have been greater than has recently been felt in the eastern part of this state by a few copies of this perishable production . . . When an old Negro from Boston writes a book and sends it among us, the whole country is thrown into commotion."

The commotion reached unprecedented proportions. The legislatures of several Southern states went into secret sessions to consider Walker's *Appeal*, and the mayor of Savannah, Georgia, asked the mayor of Boston to arrest Walker and suppress his book. More sinister yet were reports of rewards for Walker's death. Friends, fearing for his safety, urged him to flee to Canada. But Walker refused, saying: "If any are anxious to ascertain who I am, know the world, that I am one of the oppressed, degraded and wretched sons of Africa, rendered so by the avaricious and unmerciful, among the whites. — If any wish to plunge me into the wretched incapacity of a slave, or murder me for the truth, know ye, that I am in the hands of God, and at your disposal. I count my life not dear unto me, but I am ready to be offered at any moment. For what is the use of living, when in fact I am dead."

A few months later, on June 28, 1830, Walker was found dead near the doorway of his store. His supporters said he had been poisoned by racists or agents of racists.

In this way or some other way, the pen of the gifted and impassioned prophet was stilled. But the bell of his words continued to ring, and the echo was heard in distant places.

A BURNING
for a
BURNING

————————◆————————

Nat Turner

> *...thou shalt give life for life, eye for eye,*
> *tooth for tooth, hand for hand, foot for foot,*
> *burning for burning.*
>
> **EXODUS**

NAT TURNER was David Walker's word made flesh.

One year after Walker's death and 134 years before Watts, Nat Turner and a band of black rebels cut a swath of blood through the sleepy little Virginia county of Southampton. For forty-eight hours, Nat held Southampton County in a black embrace of death. For forty-eight hours, he and his men hacked and maimed white flesh. When, at length, the insurrection ended, fifty-seven white persons lay dead and the gaping wound of slavery lay open for all to see.

In this effort, the largest and bloodiest slave revolt in American history, Nat Turner made slavery serious. After Nat's insurrection, it was no longer possible for men to pretend. There were men in the slave quarters. One could not always depend on their masks. At any moment, the mask could turn into a horrid face of blood and vengeance.

Nat Turner illuminated the shadows of slavery and his revolt opened a raging national debate which led link by link to the militant abolitionists, John Brown, and the Civil War. "No ante-bellum Southerner," Kenneth Stampp writes, "could ever forget Nat Turner. The career of this man made an impact upon the people of his section as great as that of John C. Calhoun or Jefferson Davis."

The man who made this impact on the South was a black

slave who has not yet received his due in history. He has been presented to history by white authors who libeled him and distorted his deeds. But despite libels and distortions, Nat Turner still sears the subconscious of the nation, because the gaping wound he opened still runs.

The prototype of twentieth century revolutionaries, Nat Turner reminds us that oppression is a kind of violence which pays in coins of its own minting. He reminds us that the first and greatest of all gospels is this: that individuals and social systems always reap what they sow.

One cannot understand Turner without understanding the reality he revealed and rejected. That reality was American slavery, one of the cruellest social systems designed by man. This system was designed to destroy the black man. The American slave was denied freedom of thought and freedom of movement. The slaves — male and female — belonged body and soul to their master. It was true, literally true, that black men and women had no rights white men were bound to respect.

In this situation, it was ludicrous to speak of kindness. For the only way a master could be kind to a slave was to cease being a master. And the only way a slave could be true to himself and to mankind was to stop being a slave.

Contrary to the common impression, American slavery was a grimy business that spared neither the master nor slave. Conflict did not grow out of their situation; conflict was inherent in the situation. That which was human in the slave was always at war with that in the master which breached the bounds of the human.

Frederick Douglass, the former slave and black abolitionist, put his finger on the heart of the matter — the abrogation of the social contract by slavemasters. He was, he said, "a slave of society, which has, in fact, in form and substance, bound itself to assist the white man in robbing me of my rightful liberty and the just rewards of my labor." As a result, Douglass said, "whatever rights I have against the master, I have equally against those confederated with him in robbing me of my liberty. Since society has marked me out as privileged plunder, on the principle of self-preservation, I am justified in plundering in turn."

Almost all slaves internalized this viewpoint. They did not feel that they had unqualified moral obligations to whites — and whites knew it. It was considered right and proper to steal from whites and to lie to them. In an ironic reversal of the Taney dictum, slaves acted as though white people had no rights they were bound to respect — if they were clever enough, and quick enough.

Nat Turner was born into this human hell, this circle of shadows and sorcery and blood. He came into a world that defined him violently and there was no other way for him to define himself except in reaction to that violence. He had either to meet it, to run away from it, or to deform himself by conforming to it. That much was clear from the day of his birth.

He was born on October 2, 1800 — the same year as the abortive Virginia slave rebellion by Gabriel Prosser. His mother, an African-born slave, could not bear the idea of bringing another slave into the world, and she was so enraged at his birth that she had to be tied to keep her from murdering him.

Nat came soon to passion. Early in life, he came to the view that God had set him aside for some great purpose. "In my childhood," he said later, "a circumstance occurred which made an indelible impression on my mind, and laid the groundwork of that enthusiasm, which has terminated so fatally to many. . . . Being at play with other children, when three or four years old, I was telling them something, which my mother overhearing, said it had happened before I was born — I stuck to my story, however, and related some things which went, in her opinion, to confirm it — others being called on were greatly astonished, knowing that these things had happened, and caused them to say in my hearing, I surely would be a prophet, as the Lord had shown me things that had happened before my birth. And my father and mother strengthened me in this my first impression, saying in my presence, I was intended for some great purpose, which they had always thought from certain marks on my head and breast. . . . My grandmother, who was very religious, and to whom I was much attached — my master, who belonged to the church, and other religious persons who visited the house, and whom I often saw at prayers, noticing the singularity of my manners, I suppose, and my uncommon intelligence for a child, remarked I had too much sense to be raised, and, if I was, I would never be of any service to any one as a slave."

Nat was a precocious child with a restless, inquisitive, observant mind. His mother and father taught him to read, "and this learning," he said, "was constantly improved at all opportunities when I got large enough to go to work, while employed, I was reflecting on many things that would present themselves to my imagination, and whenever an opportunity occurred of looking at a book, when the school children were getting their lessons, I would find many things that the fertility of my own imagination had depicted to me before." Then and later, Nat said his mind was principally occupied by religious sentiments but "there was nothing that I saw or heard of to which my attention was not directed." He added: ". . . all my time, not devoted to my master's service, was spent either in prayer, or in making experiments in casting different things in moulds made of earth, in attempting to make paper, gunpowder, and many other experiments . . ."

Some white writers have tried to divorce Nat from the circle of blackness which sustained him from childhood to death. But Nat tells us that he was one with his people. He tells us that he grew up "among them" and that "such was the confidence of the Negroes in the neighborhood even at this early period of my life, in my superior judgment, that they would often carry me with them when they were going on any roguery to plan for them."

It was about this time that Nat's father, a fearless and freedom-loving man, ran away from his master and escaped to the North. This event undoubtedly made a vivid impression on young Nat who began to prepare himself for the great mission of his life. He forswore tobacco, liquor, and material things; and the austerity of his life and manners "became the subject of remark by white and black." Thomas Gray, a local lawyer who interviewed Nat in prison and edited the first *Confessions of Nat Turner*, said: "It is notorious, that he was never known to have a dollar in his life, to swear an oath, or drink a drop of spirits."

Nat played on the sensibilities of Gray and other contemporaries by wrapping himself in mystery. As he explained later: "Having soon discovered to be great, I must appear so, and therefore studiously avoided mixing in society, and wrapped myself in mystery, devoting my time to fasting and prayer. By this time, having arrived to man's estate, and hearing the scriptures commented on at meetings, I was struck with that particular passage which says: 'Seek ye the kingdom of Heaven and all things shall be added unto you.' I reflected much on this passage, and prayed daily for light on this subject ... As I was praying one day at my plough, the spirit spoke to me, saying 'Seek ye the kingdom of Heaven and all things shall be added unto you.' ... And for two years I prayed continually, whenever my duty would permit — and then again I had the same revelation, which fully confirmed me in the impression that I was ordained for some great purpose in the hands of the Almighty. Several years rolled round, in which many events occurred to strengthen me in this belief. At this time I reverted in my mind to the remarks made of me in my childhood, and the things that had been shown me — and as it had been said of me in my childhood by those by whom I had been taught to pray, both whites and black, and in whom I had the greatest confidence, that I had too much sense to be raised, and if I was, I would never be of any use to any one as a slave. Now finding I had arrived to man's estate, and was a slave, and these revelations being made known to me, I began to direct my attention to this great object, to fulfil the purpose for which, by this time, I felt assured I was intended."

A mystic with blood on his mind, a preacher with vengeance on his lips, a dreamer, a fanatic, a terrorist, Nat Turner was a fantastic mixture of gentleness, ruthlessness, and piety. Of middling stature, black in color, in demeanor bold and commanding, he was a familiar and respected figure in Southampton County which was near the southeastern border of Virginia. In 1831, there were 9,500 slaves and 6,500 whites in the county which was, as Thomas Wentworth Higginson observed, a "rural, lethargic, slipshod Virginia neighborhood, with the due allotment of mansion-houses and log huts, tobacco-fields and 'old fields,' horses, dogs, Negroes, 'poor white folks,' so called, and other white folks, poor without being called so." The county seat was Jerusalem, a mere slip of a town some seventy miles from Norfolk and Richmond and about fifteen miles from "The Cross Keys," the small community where Nat lived.

Nat Turner came to maturity in this community. He married a black slave woman and became a father. He also went through the usual temptations, the temptation of doubt — the gnawing doubt of oneself, of one's cause, of one's people — the temptation of despair, the tendency to say, "What's the use, why bother, there's no way out;" and the greatest temptation of all, the temptation of success within the system. By keeping his mouth shut and saying yes at the right time, Nat Turner could have become a driver or perhaps an overseer. He could have whipped other slaves. He could have become the slave-in-charge, and white people could have used him to justify the system. But Nat had too much integrity for this trap. He immersed himself in religion, seeking yet another way out, personal salvation up yonder.

In Nat's day, as in this one, Christianity was used, with notable exceptions, to justify the violence of rich white people against poor nonwhite peoples. It was used to tell barefoot people that they were going to get shoes in Heaven.

This missionary version of Christianity, which was drilled into the minds of the slaves, repelled Nat. In the Old Testament, in the blood-and-doom passages, he found a corroboration of his manhood; and in the New Testament he found a despised man, a racial outcast, a poor man, a *revolutionary* who cursed fig trees and violently drove money-changers from profaned temples.

Consumed by the images and the visions of the Old and New Testament, Nat Turner turned the Book against the people who had given it to him. The more Nat read the Bible, the more he became convinced that he was destined to lead his people out of slavery. Like Joan of Arc, he had provocative visions of the impending doom of his adversaries. He heard voices and he saw visions. He saw drops of blood on the corn in the field, and he saw "white spirits and black spirits engaged in battle, and the sun was darkened—the thunder rolled in the Heavens, and blood flowed in streams—and I heard a voice saying, 'Such is your luck, such you are called to see, and let it come rough or smooth, you must surely bear it.'"

In the violent visions that lashed him, a destiny opened up before Nat Turner and he knew it was his destiny. Nonetheless, he fought against that destiny, for he was not a violent man. He asked God, who spoke to him in the woods and fields and while he labored at the plow, to let that cup pass from him. But God pressed, and Nat fled, running away from his master and spending thirty days in the wilderness.

A Burning for a Burning

It was here that Nat overcame his last temptation—the temptation to escape to the free colonies of Canada. But individual escape was a personal solution and the spirit called Nat to a collective solution. In the wilderness, Nat rejected the solution of individual escape.

Now, in despair, Nat looked violence full in the face. What he thought can be inferred from what he did. And what he did suggests that he had plumbed the depths of the dynamics of oppression—which is not as complex as some people pretend.

In the dynamics of oppression, there are four stages of violence and all these stages are different moments of the original act of violence. In the original act of violence, one group lays violent hands on another group and reduces it to submission and degradation. This original violence is sustained and perpetuated by institutions (armies, police forces) which are designed to maintain in being the thefts of the original violence.

Once this happens, once violence is imposed on a situation and perpetuated by violent institutions, the situation itself and all the participants in the situation are defined by violence. Violence becomes the ambience of their being, and it whirls around and around within them, touching everything and sparing nothing.

In the second stage of oppression, the oppressed group internalizes the original violence of the oppressors. If the oppressed group finds no instrument, violent or nonviolent, for turning this violence from themselves, they inevitably turn this violence upon themselves, killing and maiming each other in rites of self-destruction. In Nat Turner's day, as in our own, the internalized violence of the system came out in many ways: in violent language, in the frenzies of religion and dancing and sex, in the despairing acts of emasculated men who whipped their wives because the massed violence of the system prevented them from whipping their tormentors.

What I am concerned to emphasize here is that the violence

90

that flows out of a system of oppression is merely the objective violence of the system itself. To be quite precise, I am saying that the violence of Nat Turner was the reflected violence of Nat Turner's oppressors.

That point is a key to an understanding of Nat Turner. A child of violence, he became a transmission belt of violence in an abortive attempt to free all men from violence. And in that attempt he emphasized the third law of violence—and that law is that violence always rebounds, always returns home. Nat Turner's revolt was the violence of the slaveowner turned back on the slaveowner. It was the oppressor's violence boomeranging and returning home.

And, of course, this brought into play the fourth moment of violence, an intensification of the original violence, a multiplication of the instruments designed to suppress the slaves. Thus the violence of the system closed in on itself, contradicting itself. And in the process the system cracked under the internal strain.

Did Nat Turner see all this?

The record suggests that he saw part of it and acted out the rest. Philosophy apart, Nat saw that it was necessary for the oppressed to confront the violence of the system directly. He saw that it was necessary for his people to seek out the source of their anguish and smash it. He was obsessed by one idea: the destruction of all masters. In his view, the enemy was society. The only solution, he believed, was a war of extermination and the creation of a new society in America.

All his life, he had been preparing for this task and now, in the year of 1828, he was almost ready. On May 12 of that year, Nat said he "heard a loud noise in the heavens, and the Spirit instantly appeared to me and said the Serpent was loosened, and Christ had laid down the yoke he had borne for the sins of men, and that I should take it on and fight against the Serpent, for the time was fast approaching when the first should be the last and the last should be first." The Spirit told Nat that a sign would appear in the heavens and that "on the appearance of the sign, I should arise and prepare myself, and slay my enemies with their own weapons." The sign Nat sought appeared with an eclipse of the sun in February, 1831. "And immediately on the sign appearing in the heavens," Nat said, "the seal was removed from my lips. . . ."

Nat, who was thirty, immediately chose four disciples — Henry, Hark, Nelson, and Sam — and set his face toward Jerusalem. He resolved to strike on July 4, but he became ill and the day passed. There then came another sign, the peculiar color of the sun of August 13, 1831. Nat set another date: Sunday, August 21.

On the appointed day, Nat and his disciples gathered on the banks of a pond on the property of his master, a luckless white named Joseph Travis. Nat, who knew the value of a dramatic entrance, arrived late and found two new recruits — Will and Jack. "I saluted them on coming up," Nat said, "and asked Will how came he there. He answered, his life was worth no more than others, and his liberty as dear to him. I asked him if he thought to obtain it? He said he would or lose his life. That was enough to put him in full confidence." Will, who was the slave of a sadistic master, kept his word. In fact, he wielded the broadax with such ferocity that he became the unofficial executioner of the group.

Having assured himself of the determination and loyalty of his men, Nat outlined his plans. They would strike that night, he said, beginning at the house of his master and proceeding from house to house, killing every man, woman, and child. In this way, he explained, they would terrorize the whites and sap their will. Then, Nat said, women and children would be spared and men "too, who ceased to resist."

What was his ultimate objective?

Nobody knows for sure. It seems that he intended to precipitate a general slave rebellion and capture the state. In the event of failure, he probably intended to retreat to the Dismal Swamp and fight a Castro-style guerilla war.

It was about ten o'clock when Nat and his disciples embarked on their mission, and Southampton County was dark and still. The rebels—armed with one hatchet and a broadax—moved silently and swiftly through the darkness to the home of Joseph Travis, Nat's master. "Hark got a ladder," Nat says, "and set it against the chimney, on which I ascended, and hoisting a window, entered and came down stairs, unbarring the door, and removed the guns from their places. It was then observed that I must spill the first blood. On which, armed with a hatchet, and accompanied by Will, I entered my master's chamber, it becoming dark, I could not give a death blow, the hatchet glanced from his head, he sprang from the bed and called his wife, it was his last word, Will laid him dead, with a blow of his axe, and Mrs. Travis shared the same fate, as she lay in bed. The murder of this family, five in number, was the work of a moment, not one of them awoke...." An infant, sleeping in a cradle, was spared. As the group left the house, Nat ordered Will and Henry to return and kill the infant. "Nits," he said, "make lice."

At the Travis house, the rebels appropriated four guns, several old muskets, and a pound or two of powder. "We remained some time," Nat said, "at the barn, where we paraded; I formed them in a line as soldiers, and after carrying them through all the maneuvers I was master of, marched them off to Mr. Salathul Frances', about six hundred yards distant. Sam and Will went to the door and knocked. Mr. Francis asked who was there, Sam replied it was him, and he had a letter for him, on which he got up and came to the door, they immediately seized him, and dragging him out a little from the door, he was dispatched by repeated blows on the head; there was no other white person in the family. We started from there for Mrs. Reese's, maintaining the most perfect silence on our march, where finding the door unlocked, we entered, and murdered Mrs. Reese in her bed, while sleeping; her son awoke, but it was only to sleep the sleep of death, he had only time to say who is that, and he was no more. From Mrs. Reese's we went to Mrs. Turner's, a mile distant, which we reached about sunrise, on Monday morning. Henry, Austin, and Sam, went to the still, where, finding Mr. Peebles, Austin shot him, and the rest of us went to the house; as we approached, the family discovered us, and shut the door. Vain hope! Will, with one stroke of his axe, opened it, and we entered and found Mrs. Turner and Mrs. Newsome in the middle of the room, almost frightened to death. Will immediately killed Mrs. Turner, with one blow of his axe. I took Mrs. Newsome by the hand, and with the sword I had when I was apprehended, I struck her several blows over the head, but not being able to kill her, as the sword was dull. Will turning around and discovering it, dispatched her also. A general destruction of property and search for money and ammunition, always succeeded the murders. By this time my company amounted to fifteen, and nine men mounted, who started for Mrs. Whitehead's, (the other six were to go through a by way to Mr. Bryant's, and rejoin us at Mrs. Whitehead's) as we approached the house we discovered Mr. Richard Whitehead standing in the cotton patch, near the land fence; we called him over into the lane, and Will, the executioner, was near at hand, with his fatal axe, to send him to an untimely grave. As we pushed on to the house, I discovered someone run round the garden, and thinking it was some of the white family, I pursued them, but finding it was a servant girl belonging to the house, I returned to commence the work of death, but they whom I left, had not been idle; all the family were already murdered, but Mrs. Whitehead and her daughter Margaret. As I came round to the door I saw Will pulling Mrs. Whitehead out of the house, and at the step he nearly severed her head from her body, with his broad axe. Miss Margaret, when I discovered her, had concealed herself in the corner, formed by the projection of the cellar cap from the house; on my approach she fled, but was soon overtaken, and after repeated blows with a sword, I killed her by a blow on the head, with a fence rail."

By this time, the first bodies had been discovered and a nameless dread seized the white citizens. Women, children, and men fled to the woods and hid under leaves. Some men left the county; others left the state.

Nat rode on, picking up slave recruits at almost every stop, chopping down old, young, male, female. No one with a white skin was spared except a family of poor whites who owned no slaves.

"I took my station in the rear," Nat said, "and as it was my object to carry terror and devastation wherever we went, I placed fifteen or twenty of the best armed and most to be relied on, in front, who generally approached the houses as fast as their horses could run, this was for two purposes, to prevent their escape and strike terror to the inhabitants — on this account I never got to the houses, after leaving Mrs. Whitehead's, until the murders were committed, except in one case. I sometimes got in sight in time to see the work of death completed, viewed the mangled bodies as they lay, in silent satisfaction...."

By now, Nat commanded some sixty men, "all mounted and armed with guns, axes, swords and clubs." More importantly, he was within three miles of Jerusalem, his main objective. But it was at this point, when he was in striking distance of success, that Nat made his first major mistake. Against his better judgment, he permitted his men to stop at the home of James W. Parker. The men, some of whom were groggy from periodic raids on cider stills, tarried. Nat left a detachment at the gate of the farm and started to the house to get them. At this precise moment, eighteen whites approached with drawn guns. Nat ordered a charge. The whites held their ground for a moment and then retreated in disorder. Nat gave chase, crossed a hill and discovered a larger group of whites. Nat retreated, retracing his steps and recruiting additional men. The next day he was defeated and his men dispersed. After a vain effort to rally his troops, Nat gave up, dug a cave and went into hiding.

By this time, soldiers were flocking to Southampton County from all points. All in all, some three thousand armed men, federal and state, came to the county to put down the insurrection. Enraged by the boldness of the blacks, the soldiers and militiamen massacred scores of innocent blacks.

Nat eluded capture for almost two months. But he was seized finally and carried to Jerusalem. He refused to plead guilty at his trial, saying that he did not feel so. But he was found guilty and sentenced by Judge Jeremiah Cobb who said: "The judgment of the court is, that you be taken hence to the jail, from whence you came, thence to the place of execution, and on Friday next, between the hours of 10 A.M. and 2 P.M. be hung by the neck until you are dead! dead! dead! . . . ."

In death as in life, Nat Turner was an example to his oppressors. Until the end, he was calm and cool, sure of his act and the eventual vindication of history. Thomas Gray said: "The calm, deliberate composure with which he spoke of his late deeds and intentions, the expression of his fiend-like face when excited by enthusiasm, still bearing the stains of the blood of helpless innocence about him; clothed in rags and covered with chains, yet daring to raise his manacled hands to heaven, with a spirit soaring above the attributes of man; I looked on him and my blood curdled in my veins."

On November 11, 1831, a white man with a rope broke Nat Turner's neck on a gallows in a town in Virginia called Jerusalem. But ideas cannot be killed with ropes. The idea Nat Turner represented — the idea of black liberation — lived on in the generation of crisis Nat Turner's insurrection brought to a head. The Turner insurrection, author W. S. Drewry wrote, "was a landmark in the history of slavery.... It was the forerunner of the great slavery debates, which resulted in the abolition of slavery in the United States and was, indirectly, most instrumental in bringing about this result. Its importance is truly conceived by the old Negroes of Southampton and vicinity, who reckon all time from 'Nat's Fray' or 'Old Nat's War.'"

WHITE *on* BLACK

—◄►—

Wendell Phillips
and
William Lloyd Garrison

*I can never forget — I never wish to forget,
the long years I have been permitted to serve
the Negro race. The poor, poor Negro, who
never yet leaned on the word of a white man
without finding it a broken reed....*

WENDELL PHILLIPS

WENDELL PHILLIPS and *WILLIAM LLOYD GARRISON*

AMERICA WAS ablaze with agitation.

Demonstrators were going to prison in droves, and men and women were tramping the streets, singing freedom songs. There were sit-ins, freedom rides, long hot summers, and fights over *de facto* segregation. "Good people" were fulminating over bearded white youth who kept the community astir with demonstrations for black freedom. And a remarkable man, considered by some the conscience of the age, was preaching the virtues of love and passive resistance.

These events, so modern in tone and texture, unfolded in America more than one hundred years ago.

The prototypal freedom fighters were abolitionists who provoked an apathetic people into facing the greatest moral issue of their times.

The pioneer apostle of nonviolence was William Lloyd Garrison, a fiery white editor who shared leadership of the militant abolitionist wing with several black and white radicals, including Wendell Phillips, the Boston blueblood who gave up place and position and dedicated himself heart and soul to the struggle for black rights.

Few white men anywhere have been as dedicated to black freedom as Garrison, Phillips, and their abolitionist followers. Garrison, the brilliant editor, and Phillips, the eloquent orator, were leading actors in the movement which led to the freeing of the black slave and enactment of the Fourteenth and Fifteenth amendments. Forsaking all others, identifying themselves totally with the Afro-American, sparing neither friend nor foe, Garrison and Phillips created an indigenous white radical tradition, which echoes today in the words and deeds of white students and adults attached to the second Freedom movement.

The two Boston reformers were symbols of an age of reform and rebellion. In the first three decades of the nineteenth century, America was convulsed by wave after wave of reforms, focusing now on prisons, now on schools, now on women's underwear (the Amelia Bloomer crusade). Overshadowing all, subtly shaping and distending all, was a surge of religious enthusiasm which spilled over into the antislavery crusade. This crusade, which started long before Garrison and Phillips were born, was confined largely to the area of innocuous humanitarianism until the latter part of the 1820's and the appearance of radical black agitators like David Walker and militant black newspapers like *Freedom's Journal*.

Both Garrison and Phillips were steeped from birth in the fermenting tensions and enthusiasms of the age. Garrison, who ran the first leg of the race that Phillips carried to a logical conclusion, was born on December 10, 1805, the son of a hard-drinking seaman who wandered off one day and was never heard from again. The future reformer grew up in abject poverty, scrounging for food on the streets of Newburyport, a seacoast community about forty miles north of Boston. Apprenticed to an editor at the age of thirteen, he educated himself and became an expert printer and a writer. By 1826, at the age of twenty-one, he was editor of a radical local paper. When this paper failed, he moved on to Boston where he came under the influence of Benjamin Lundy, a pioneer antislavery editor. Beginning on the right as an advocate of Lundy's program of gradual emancipation and colonization, Garrison moved to the left under the influence of black agitators like

Samuel E. Cornish and David Walker. At this juncture, white advocates of black freedom were pursuing a program that would be called white liberalism today. Garrison denounced this approach and called for a crusade of total commitment. "A few white victims," he said, "must be sacrificed to open the eyes of this nation and show the tyranny of our laws. I expect and am willing to be persecuted, imprisoned and bound for advocating African rights, and I should deserve to be a slave myself if I shrunk from that duty or danger." Rejecting the liberal-humanitarian rhetoric, Garrison adopted a radical program of immediate and total emancipation. In 1830, he and Isaac Knapp, a Boston printer, resolved to publish a radical antislavery journal as long as they could subsist on bread and water. On Saturday, January 1, 1831, the first issue of Garrison's *Liberator* appeared on the streets of Boston.

"I will be as harsh as truth," Garrison announced in his first editorial, "and as uncompromising as justice. On this subject [slavery], I do not wish to think, or speak, or write, with moderation. No! No! Tell a man whose house is on fire to give a moderate alarm; tell him to moderately rescue his wife from the hands of the ravisher; tell the mother to gradually extricate her babe from the fire into which it has fallen; — but urge me not to use moderation in a cause like the present. I am in earnest — I will not equivocate — I will not excuse — I will not retreat a single inch — AND I WILL BE HEARD."

Garrison was harsh; he did not equivocate — and he was heard. By singular circumstance, black people played a major role in pushing the twenty-six-year-old editor into the national spotlight. Black people, especially James Forten, the wealthy Philadelphia manufacturer, were among the chief financial supporters of the *Liberator*. Black people also financed Garrison's sensationally successful propaganda foray into England. Of even greater importance in the transformation of Garrison into a person of national importance was the work of

103

David Walker, a free black writer, and Nat Turner, a slave insurrectionist. Two years before the publication of the *Liberator*, David Walker published his radical pamphlet. In 1831, shortly after the appearance of the *Liberator*, Nat Turner exploded in Southampton County, Virginia. Walker's words and Turner's deeds caused consternation in the South. The governors of several Southern states asked the Boston mayor to suppress the *Liberator*, which was responsible, they said, for the Walker pamphlet and the Nat Turner insurrection. Garrison was not responsible for the militancy of Nat Turner and Walker, who were a great deal more radical than he was; but he shrewdly used the notoriety as a sounding board for the propagation of his own ideas. Shortly after the Nat Turner insurrection, Garrison founded the New England Antislavery Society. The next year he played a key role in the founding of the American Antislavery Society.

With the founding of the New England and American Antislavery societies, abolitionists became an organized force capable of carrying the battle into the enemy camp. Local societies were organized and agents who lived on subsistence wages were sent out to agitate and to organize the countryside. More importantly, vigilance committees were organized to move fugitive slaves from station to station on the Underground Railroad. As a direct result of the efforts of abolitionists, slavery became a living issue in the minds of men, and the way was prepared for the Civil War.

The abolitionists came in all sizes and shapes and colors. Some championed political action; others called for passive resistance; still others called for fire and blood and steel. Of whatever persuasion, the abolitionists were totally committed. They staged sit-ins and freedom rides, and they traveled hundreds of miles organizing and agitating. Some of the more adventurous made a practice of invading churches on Sunday and launching antislavery speeches at the first lull in the ceremony. When a

New York preacher announced that slavery was "a divine institution," an abolitionist stood up and said: "So is hell!"

Most abolitionists were hard-working members of the middle and lower middle classes. But there was a fringe element of cultists. Some abolitionists expressed their defiance by growing long beards. Others chose unconventional acts of commitment. Rev. Samuel E. May said: "We abolitionists are what we are,—babes, sucklings, obscure men, silly women, publicans, sinners, and we shall manage this matter just as might be expected of such persons as we are. It is unbecoming in abler men who stood by and would do nothing to complain of us because we do no better."

As editor of the *Liberator* and as a major force in the Massachusetts and American antislavery associations, Garrison was in the forefront of the abolitionist crusade. He served primarily as a catalyst and fertilizing agent, holding up a banner of uncompromising resistance, a banner that attracted men and women as diverse in background as Frederick Douglass, the former slave, and the Grimké sisters, the Charleston, South Carolina, aristocrats who scandalized the South with their demands for black freedom. Some abolitionists deplored Garrison's enthusiasms (women's rights, peace, and passive resistance) and his attacks on structures of power (the church and the Northern business community); but almost all abolitionists were influenced by his posture. Wendell Phillips said later that Garrison influenced men who never knew that it was he who influenced them. "The public sentiment which Lincoln obeys," Archibald W. Grimké said, "[Garrison and] Phillips created."

So devoted was the Boston editor to black liberation that many people believed he was a black man, a fact that did not disturb Garrison at all. "I never rise to address a colored audience," he told a black group, "without feeling ashamed of my color; ashamed of being identified with a race of men who have done you so much injustice and yet retain so large a portion of your brethren in servitude."

Like many great reformers, Garrison was vain and autocratic. His attempts to control the thinking of his black and white colleagues kept the movement in constant turmoil. Frederick Douglass, the great black abolitionist, and several other black leaders acknowledged Garrison's contributions, but they told him in no uncertain terms that he could not define the black man's posture of protest. In 1840, after a heated controversy over one of Garrison's pet projects, equal rights for women, the abolitionist movement split into two wings, with Garrison and his adherents, blacks and whites, standing on the left.

Another Garrison plank, passive resistance, generated several controversies. Garrison was a total believer in passive resistance. He not only rejected violent instruments (arms, police forces, and armies), but he also rejected the instruments (ballots) of a system maintained by violence. Like Tolstoy, Garrison derived his passive resistance doctrines from Jesus and the New Testament. "The history of mankind," he said, "is crowded with evidence proving that physical coercion is not adapted to moral regeneration; that the sinful dispositions of men can be subdued only by love; that evil can be exterminated from the earth only by goodness; ... that there is great security in being gentle, harmless, long-suffering, and abundant in mercy, that it is only the meek who shall inherit the earth, for the violent who resort to the sword are destined to perish with the sword."

Passivity apart, resistance carried Garrison to some interesting positions. He called for a dissolution of the Union, denouncing the Constitution with its proslavery clauses as "a covenant with death and an agreement with hell." After passage of the fugitive slave bill of 1850, he burned a copy of the U.S. Constitution before a large audience and shouted: "So perish all compromises with tyranny! And let all the people say, Amen!" It is recorded that most of the people shouted: "Amen!"

Eschewing compromise, preaching sin, guilt, and repentance, Garrison trained his fire on Northerners who tolerated slavery and black degradation. Like modern crusaders, he tried to mobilize Northern public opinion against Southern atrocities. His aims were simple and direct: to startle, to disturb, to shame. Though mild and meek in his personal relations, he was harsh and passionate in the press and on the platform. A dark, balding man, near-sighted and hard of hearing, Garrison was a master of vituperation and propaganda. Criticized once for his use of fiery language, Garrison replied: "... I have need to be all on fire, for I have mountains of ice about me to melt."

Alarmed by the success of Garrison and other abolitionists, proslavery forces counterattacked, organizing riots in Northern and Southern cities. In Charleston, South Carolina, the U.S. mail was burned in an unsuccessful attempt to silence Northern "agitators." In Philadelphia, an abolitionist hall was put to the torch and black churches and an orphan home were gutted. There were anti-Negro and anti-abolitionist riots in New York, Boston, Cincinnati, and other cities. Not only hoodlums but "respectable people" mobilized to silence abolitionists who, they said, were driving a wedge between the North and the South. On one celebrated occasion, a "broadcloth" mob attacked a woman's antislavery meeting, lassoed Garrison with a rope and dragged him through the streets of Boston in his underwear.

Enter at this precise moment Wendell Phillips.

As the crowd pulled Garrison through the streets, Phillips watched with amazement. Pushing into the crowd, he called for intervention by the regiment and was told that the guards were members of the mob. Phillips walked away, thinking. Later, when he fell in love with a wealthy young abolitionist who said she would marry him only if he swore "eternal enmity" to slavery, Phillips was more than half-prepared.

The conversion of Phillips was a major turning point in the antislavery drama. Unlike Garrison, Phillips was a child of ease and comfort. Born November 29, 1811, the scion of one of New England's first families and the son of Boston's first mayor, Phillips was a graduate of Harvard College and the Harvard University Law School. It would be said later that his whole life could be compressed into one sentence: "He was born in Beacon Street and he died on Common Street."

Egged on by Ann Terry Greene, the young woman he later married, Phillips turned his back on wealth and social prominence and plunged into the antislavery movement. He received his baptism of fire in December, 1837, at a Boston mass meeting called to protest the murder of Elijah P. Lovejoy by a proslavery mob in Alton, Illinois. When the attorney general of the commonwealth shouted that Lovejoy "died as the fool dieth," Phillips strode to the platform. The crowd, swayed by a proslavery claque, was by this time overwhelmingly anti-Lovejoy; and Phillips was greeted by hisses, catcalls, and boos. The young lawyer stood his ground, cool, poised, unruffled, staring at the crowd with a disdainful contempt. Overawed by his presence, the crowd grew silent and the melodious voice that would later charm thousands was heard from a public platform for the first time. By sheer eloquence and force of personality, Phillips turned an anti-Lovejoy plurality into a pro-Lovejoy majority. The speech he gave that day was later called one of the three greatest oratorical triumphs in American history. And from that day, Wendell Phillips was hailed as "the golden voice" of abolitionism.

For more than thirty years, Phillips dominated hostile crowds with the brilliance of his manner and the coolness of his bearing. His speeches were models of simplicity and directness. Speaking in a conversational tone, never raising his voice, he introduced a new style in American oratory and he was hailed by ally and foe as the finest speaker of the day. He was at his best in a hall of hissing enemies ("Hang the nigger"), with heavy objects raining down on the platform, and the yolk of a bad egg running down the front of his frock coat. Once, when a proslavery mob stormed onto the platform with a rope to hang him, Phillips disdainfully waved them away, saying: "Wait until I tell this story."

Six feet tall, handsome, elegantly dressed, Phillips was a striking exhibit and he soon became a co-leader of the Garrisonian branch of the abolitionist movement. Like Garrison, Phillips was prepared to pay any price in the cause of freedom. He refused to practice law or perform any other duty under the Constitution until slavery was abolished. So enamored was he of black freedom that his family attempted unsuccessfully to confine him in a sanatorium as a lunatic. "If I die before emancipation," he said, "write this for my epitaph: Here lies Wendell Phillips, infidel to a church that defended human slavery — traitor to a government that was only an organized conspiracy against the rights of men."

Phillips lived his creed. He refused to ride in cars that barred black people and went hungry rather than eat in rooms that were not open to Frederick Douglass and other black abolitionists.

The New England patrician gloried in the name of agitator, choosing as the title of a Harvard Phi Beta Kappa address "The Scholar in a Republic, of Necessity an Agitator." The agitator, he said, "must stand outside of organizations, with no bread to earn, no candidate to elect, no party to save, no object but truth, — to tear a question open and riddle it with light."

Phillips supported most of the Garrisonian program, but he drew the line at passive resistance. "No," he said, "I confess I am not a non-resistant. The reason why I advise the slave to be guided by a policy of peace is because he has no chance. If he had one, — if he had as good a chance as those who went up to Lexington seventy-seven years ago, — I should call him the basest recreant that ever deserted wife and child if he did not vindicate his liberty by his own right hand...."

As the Civil War drew near, practically all abolitionists openly abandoned Garrison's passive resistance program and Phillips became the leader of the militant wing of the movement. John Brown's raid on Harpers Ferry and the firing on Fort Sumter accentuated the strains in the movement. Garrison called for national unity and denounced "minute criticisms" of Lincoln's racial program. Frederick Douglass and Phillips disagreed, calling for an intensification of antislavery propaganda. Seizing the mantle from Garrison, Phillips dashed from city to city, excoriating Lincoln and calling for the emancipation of the slave and the arming of the freedmen.

When Lincoln caught up with antislavery advocates, Phillips turned to Reconstruction, articulating a bold program of land, ballots, and freedom for blacks and poor whites. "This nation," he said, "owes the Negro not merely freedom; it owes him land, and it owes him education also. It is a debt which will disgrace us before the people if we do not pay it."

Garrison, moving to the right, dismissed Phillips' Reconstruction plan as revolutionary. When he attempted in May, 1865, to dissolve the American Antislavery Society, saying that black suffrage was not a part of the original program of the abolitionist movement, Phillips and Douglass opposed him and carried the day. Garrison resigned as president of the society and Phillips succeeded him.

With Douglass and other black leaders and the two great congressional radicals, Charles Sumner and Thaddeus Stevens, Phillips campaigned for a complete reorganization of the South and passage of the Fourteenth and Fifteenth amendments. America would not heed his call for "a new social system" in the South, but Congress passed the Fourteenth and Fifteenth amendments. On March 30, 1870, President Ulysses Grant proclaimed ratification of the Fifteenth Amendment. Ten days later, the American Antislavery Society met for the last time. Frederick Douglass said that Phillips played the key role in passage of the crucial amendment. "None have been more vigilant, clear-sighted, earnest, true and eloquent," he said. "Without office, without party, only a handful at his back, he has done more to lead and mould public opinion in favor of equal suffrage than any man I know."

With passage of the Fifteenth Amendment, the first Freedom movement came to a close. Most of the white abolitionists hurriedly quit the public arena, but Phillips remained in harness, becoming, some said, more radical with each passing year. In his old age, he denounced Southern atrocities and supported the then revolutionary demand for an eight-hour day.

Garrison was comforted in his old age by his four sons, his daughter and his grandchildren. Mellowed by age, the old reformer basked in the glow of a world which no longer found him dangerous. Phillips, who had no children, spent his winter years with his invalid wife, Ann, and his books. Having given thousands of dollars to friends and charities over the years, Phillips now found himself in pinched financial circumstances and it was necessary for him to continue as a Lyceum lecturer.

During the closing phase of the abolitionist crusade, Garrison and Phillips ceased to be personal friends. But they were reconciled later, and when Garrison died in 1879 Phillips delivered one of the principal addresses at his funeral. Five years later, on February 2, 1884, Phillips collapsed after a heart attack and died at his house on Common Street. Both Phillips and Garrison went to their graves laden with the praise of men who had once called them fools and fanatics. But they were soon pushed into the background. They were too uncomfortable; even today, they make men squirm. But the fire they started still burns. The second Freedom movement is an extended echo of their lives and of Phillips' motto which is etched in the auditorium of Wendell Phillips High School in the heart of the black community of Chicago.

Peace if possible,
But Justice at any cost.

A BLACK WOMAN

in

BATTLE

Sojourner Truth

America owes my people some of the dividends. She can afford to pay, and she must pay. I shall make them understand that there is a debt to the Negro people which they never can repay. At least then, they can make amends.

SOJOURNER TRUTH

SOJOURNER TRUTH

Life had passed her by.

She was plain, she was aging, she was black. She was alone, utterly alone, in the big city of New York. She was without resources or friends. Her family was disorganized, her marriage was shattered, her name was in disgrace — life had passed her by. Or so it seemed to Isabella Van Wagener as she looked back on her life in the spring of 1843.

Looking back, musing, Isabella began, as was her habit, to speak to God. It would be an error to say that she was praying. Isabella addressed God as one human being addresses another, arguing, demanding, bargaining. She wanted to know now why she had been born. Why had He brought her into this vale of tears? Was it to wash dishes and make beds, to tickle the vanities of men, and to bow and scrape before white people? Was that all? Was that what life was really about? In a room in a house in New York City, in the year of 1843, a black woman asked God that question.

From somewhere, from the walls, from the ceiling, from the ambience of the air, came an answer. A voice filled the room, an ethereal presence. The voice — or was she imagining things? — told Isabella Van Wagener that she was not really Isabella Van Wagener. Then who was she? The voice said there was another person within her. The voice told her who that person was and what she had to do to validate her humanity.

Isabella arose, wondering. She was at that time a maid for a white family, and she continued for several days to make beds and wash dishes. But the new person, the undefined person, burned within her. As the days passed, Isabella came to see herself as an accomplice in a shameful system of robbery and wrong. "The rich rob the poor," she said, "and the poor rob one another." Isabella decided to reject the whole system. One morning in the month of June, she went to her employer, one Mrs. Whiting, and told her she was going East.

"Why?" Mrs. Whiting asked. What business did an illiterate, penniless Negro woman have in the east?

Isabella said the Spirit was calling her.

"Bell," Mrs. Whiting said, "you are crazy."

Isabella said her name was no longer Isabella. "My name," she said, pulling herself up to her full six feet, "is Sojourner Truth. The Lord named me Sojourner because I am to travel up and down the land showing the people their sins and being a sign unto them."

Leaving the dishes unwashed and the beds unmade, Sojourner Truth walked out of the Whiting kitchen into immortality. That same morning, June 1, 1843, she walked out of the "evil city" of New York, traveling in a northeasterly direction. She was an arresting figure: tall, imperious, a colorful handkerchief on her head, a bag of clothes slung over her shoulders. She had only twenty-five cents between her and starvation, but her heart was full; and from time to time she stopped in the middle of the road to give vent to the joy that was within her. On and on she went, walking, prophesying, preaching, teaching. As she walked, year after year, her fame grew. Within a short time, she stood in the front ranks of the fighters for human rights. Today, she stands with Harriet Tubman as the archetypal image of a long line of fabulously heroic Negro women. Harriet Beecher Stowe called her the Libyan Sybil. Arthur Hull Fauset said she was "God's fool." Olive Gilbert, her first biographer, said: "Through all the scenes of her eventful life may be traced the energy of a naturally powerful mind—the fearlessness and child-like simplicity of one untrammeled by education or conventional customs—purity of character—an unflinching adherence to principle—and a native enthusiasm, which, under different circumstances, might easily have produced a Joan of Arc."

This exceptional woman, one of the few originals produced in this land, was born a slave in 1797 or thereabouts in Hurley in the Catskills in upstate New York. Her parents, Baumfree and Mau Mau Bett, were slaves of a Dutchman, Colonel Hardenbergh; and they and their children spoke a Dutch brogue. Slavery was designed to destroy black males, and it soon sucked the spirit out of Baumfree. Mau Mau Bett, who was not under the same pressures, withered under the slave system; but she retained a sense of expectancy, and her passion, especially her religious mysticism, took deep roots in the soul of Isabella, the youngest save one of her ten or twelve boys and girls.

At the death of Colonel Hardenbergh, Mau Mau Bett's children were sold at auction. Isabella, a mere slip of a girl, brought only one hundred dollars. Her purchaser was John Nealy, who had a farm nearby. Nealy and his wife were cruel people, who whipped the small girl savagely.

It grieved Baumfree to see his daughter treated so. Rousing himself from his apathy, Baumfree persuaded another family to buy his daughter. The deal was consummated for one hundred and five dollars, and Isabella became a ward of the Scrivers, a hard-drinking, hard-swearing family who owned a tavern. During this interlude, she acquired a choice vocabulary of four-letter words and an unconventional approach to life. Isabella was later introduced to an entirely different style of life at the home of John J. Dumont, a well-to-do plantation owner who bought her for about three hundred dollars. By this time, Isabella was a big strapping teenager. She was soon married to a fellow slave, Thomas, who was older than his bride. Isabella had five children, but it seems that some, if not all, of her children were fathered by John J. Dumont, her master.

Even at this early date, Isabella was a person of considerable complexity. Mystical and withdrawn, she was considered a "white folks' nigger" by the other slaves. This did not, on any account, endear her to white people, who sensed something deep, something untamed and untamable, in the tall, black girl with the hypnotic eyes. It is not without significance that Isabella was loathed, generally speaking, by white women. John Dumont's wife went out of her way to make the comely slave girl's life miserable. Mrs. Dumont delighted in contriving situations that put Isabella in the wrong. She would then demand that her husband whip the recalcitrant girl.

Caught in a crossfire of fears and phobias, Isabella retreated further into herself. There was an islet on a small stream on the Dumont property. There, in a cove lined by tall willows, Isabella sought solace, pouring out her troubles to God and developing, quite by accident, the powerful speaking style that later made her one of the giants of the antislavery crusade.

In 1826, about a year before her scheduled emancipation under New York's gradual emancipation law, Isabella ran away from her master, leaving her husband and all but one of her children. The Van Wageners, a family of Quakers, took her in and later satisfied the monetary claims of her master. Isabella adopted the last name of her benefactors and started working in the neighborhood as a domestic.

It was during this period that Isabella discovered Jesus. Though she had a uniquely personal relationship with God, she had never attended a church service and had little or no knowledge of the intricacies of the Christian faith. Characteristically, she came to Jesus not through other people's words but through a personal experience.

A longing came over her one day for the old ways, and she

decided to return to Dumont. But, at the last moment, God intervened "with all the suddenness of a flash of lightning," showing her that He was everywhere "and that there was no place God was not." Isabella stopped immediately and cried out: "Oh God, I did not know you were so big." Meditating on this fact, Isabella concluded that she was too small to approach God, and she cried out for an interceder. At that moment, according to her, a space opened between her and God, and a man appeared.

"Who *are* you?" she exclaimed, adding: "I *know* you, and I *don't* know you."

As she repeated these words, she said later, the vision crystallized into a recognizable form, and she shouted: "It is Jesus. Yes, it is Jesus."

Armed now with the "power of the Lord," Isabella turned to face the world, her heart bursting with joy. She saw Jesus, she said, "as a friend standing between men and God, through whom love flowed as from a fountain." Hereafter, wherever she spoke, she would always choose as the text of her talk: "When I found Jesus."

Despite, or perhaps because of, her celebrated vision, Isabella was still seeking light. Nothing indicates this more clearly than her experiences in New York City, to which she moved in 1829, with her son, Peter. Isabella immediately joined the AME Zion Church on Church Street. But she also became a maid and supporter of Elijah Pierson, a talented religious fanatic who believed he was Elias "the Tishbite" who had been ordered to gather "the members of Israel at the foot of Mount Carmel," which he understood to mean Bowery Hill in New York.

To make things even more complicated, Robert Matthews appeared on the scene. Matthews was a Gentile who said he was a Jew. He had been converted while shaving. Sitting one day before the mirror, with the Bible balanced on his knee, he was suddenly struck by a passage. Putting down the soap, Matthews shouted: "I have found it! I have found a text which proves that no man who shaves his beard can be a true Christian." Matthews immediately threw away his razor and abandoned his name, becoming Matthias the Jew. In 1830, he prophesied the imminent destruction of Albany, New York. This event failed to come to pass, but Matthias fled and settled in New York City, where he and Pierson discovered that they were "kindred spirits." Matthias succeeded in convincing Pierson, Isabella, and several other New Yorkers, some of them hard-headed businessmen with large holdings, that he was God, or, at least, the embodiment of the Divine Presence on earth. A new community was organized with Matthias as God the Father and Pierson as John the Baptist. Since, as Matthias said, "all things [were to be held] in common," members of the group, Isabella included, withdrew their savings from banks and put the money at Matthias' disposal.

Regally turned out now in an elegant robe with twelve tassels, representing, he said, the twelve tribes of Israel, Matthias announced that it was time to establish a "New Jerusalem." With this purpose in mind, members of the community, including Benjamin Folger, a prominent New York businessman, repaired to Sing Sing, New York. Matthias, who was never at a loss for ideas, now announced the doctrine of "matched spirits." Every individual, he said, had a "match-soul," and every individual had a right, nay, a duty, to dissolve a profane marriage on meeting his "match-soul." There was method in Matthias' madness. Not too much time passed before Matthias "discovered" that he and the attractive Mrs. Folger were "match-souls." This astounding discovery was accepted with equanimity by Mr. Folger and other members of the community, and Matthias and Mrs. Folger became soul-mates. There then followed an extraordinary ritual in which different members of the community sought their soul-mates. The whole thing became extremely complicated and riotously carnal. The only person not involved in these experiments, it seems, was Isabella. But this, Isabella frankly pointed out, was not due to strength of character. It was impossible to match her soul in the "New Jerusalem."

Things went from bad to worse in Matthias' heaven on earth. Pierson became seriously ill with what seemed to be epileptic seizures. Matthias grandly refused the services of a doctor, and Pierson died. Suspicious relatives demanded an autopsy, and traces of arsenic were found. The "New Jerusalem" dissolved at this point amid flaming headlines of murder and sexual irregularities. Matthias was arrested, tried, and acquitted. Isabella was not directly implicated in the case, which was a *cause célèbre* of the day, but she figured prominently in the accounts of Benjamin Folger, who was now reconciled with his wife. Isabella sued Folger for slander. After sifting all the evidence, the jury found that Isabella was not involved in the shady goings-on at "New Jerusalem." In an astounding development for that day and age, the black woman was awarded damages against the prominent white businessman.

A little richer, and a great deal wiser, Isabella picked up the threads of her life. Her son, who had been somewhat neglected, to put it mildly, had fallen in with evil companions and was headed for ruin. After several minor involvements with the police, he was persuaded by friends to go to sea, where he disappeared without a trace.

It was at this point that Isabella decided to leave the "Babylon" of New York. Casting off her name and her old identity, she became Sojourner Truth and headed for New England. She walked for miles, stopping for the night wherever she could find a lodging place, with the rich or the poor, the saved or the damned. From time to time she took a job, accepting only enough money "to enable [her] to pay tribute to Caesar." On her trip East, Sojourner attended whatever religious meeting was at hand. But as her confidence grew, she began to hold meetings of her own. At these meetings, she sang and spoke, oftentimes reducing audiences to tears.

During this period, Sojourner put together a systematic and wholly original view of the world. Although she never learned to read or write, her original interpretations of the Bible and of constitutional law stumped seminarians and lawyers. "You read books," she was given to saying, "but God himself *talks* to me."

It was Sojourner's custom to pay adults to read the Bible to her. But she soon abandoned this practice. Adults insisted on reading *and* interpreting, and interpretation was precisely what Sojourner did not want. She later hit upon the stratagem of asking children to read to her. They did not interpret, and they did not question her habit of asking them to read a single line over and over until her mind had cracked the shell off its meaning.

After settling in Northampton, Massachusetts, where she lived for a number of years, the preacher-prophet became an antislavery advocate and a champion of women's rights. Leaving her new home in the late forties, she began a series of tours that made her a leader of the feminist and antislavery cause. A proslavery Northerner, an Ohioan, told her once: "Old woman, do you think your talk about slavery does any good?" Do you suppose that people care what you say?...Why, I don't care any more for your talk than I do for the bite of a flea."

"Perhaps not," Sojourner replied, "but the good Lord willing, I'll keep you scratching."

Sojourner Truth kept them scratching, from one end of the country to another. A powerful speaker with a deep, almost masculine, voice that could fill the largest hall, she held audiences with striking imagery and mind-seizing metaphors. Speaking once at a meeting in an area suffering from a boll weevil blight, she made a searching analysis of the U. S. Constitution. "Children," she said, "I talk to God and God talks to me. I go out and talks to God in the fields and the woods. This morning I was walking out, and I got over the fence. I saw the wheat a-holding up its head, looking very big. I go up and take holt of it. You b'lieve it, there was *no* wheat there. I say, 'God, what is the matter with *this* wheat?' And He says to me, 'Sojourner, there is a little weasel [weevil] in it!' Now I hear talkin' about the Constitution and the rights of man. I come up and I take hold of this Constitution. It looks mighty big, and I feel for my rights, but there ain't any there. Then I say 'God what ails this Constitution?' He says to me, 'Sojourner, there is a little weasel in it.'"

As the first black woman to become an antislavery speaker, Sojourner was fair game for hecklers and hoodlums. Proslavery sentiment was rife then in Illinois, Ohio, and Indiana, where Sojourner and other black speakers ran a gauntlet of brickbats and verbal volleys. The virulence of proslavery Northerners reached its height one night in northern Indiana. When Sojourner rose to address a meeting at the United Brethren community house, one Dr. Strain leaped to his feet with an objection. Some people, he said, were under the impression that Sojourner was a man masquerading as a woman. What did he propose? He suggested that a female member of the audience take Sojourner backstage and undress her. This suggestion precipitated a wild uproar. All over the floor, men and women were on their feet, yelling and screaming. The only calm figure in the hall was Sojourner Truth, who dropped her bonnet on the floor and walked to the front of the platform.

"My breasts," Sojourner shouted, "have suckled many a white babe, even when they should have been suckling my own. Some of these white babes are now grown men, and even though they have suckled my Negro breasts, they are in my opinion far more manly than any of you appear to be."

Suddenly, without preamble, Sojourner ripped open the front of her dress. "I will show my breasts to the entire congregation," she cried. "It is not my shame but yours that I should do this. Here, then, see for yourselves."

Sojourner shot out a long bony finger and stabbed the doubting doctor.

"Do you," she asked, "wish also to suck?"

Of like spirit and quality, though more rhetorical, was Sojourner's triumph at the second annual convention of the women's suffrage movement. At this convention, which was held in Akron, Ohio, in 1852, Sojourner was held at arm's length by alleged friends and avowed foes. The latter insisted that the cause of women's rights would be injured if it were coupled in the public's mind with black liberation. The result was an unspoken agreement that Sojourner would not be permitted to speak. If Sojourner was aware of all this, and she undoubtedly was, she gave no sign. Between sessions, she moved among the delegates selling copies of her autobiography, which was published in 1850. At other times, she slouched in a corner near the platform, her eyes tiredly closed, her mind apparently many miles away. As it happened, the feminists were taking a shellacking from the opposition. One man ridiculed the idea of equal rights, citing the weakness of women who had to be helped into carriages and could not carry their share of manual labor. Another speaker, a minister, said that facts were facts, and the fact was that women had made no contribution to the development of religion with, of course, the possible exception of Eve, of whom the less said the better.

At this moment, a huge black presence began unfolding near the platform. A moment or so passed before the audience realized what was happening. Then scores of women leaped to their feet, hissing and screaming: "Don't let her speak! *Don't let her speak!*"

Sojourner held her ground, and the flustered chairman finally recognized her for "a word or two." The regal black woman strode to the platform, dropped her bonnet, and turned to face the hostile audience. "Children," she said, "where there is so much racket, there must be something out of kilter."

Sojourner spun on her heels and pointed to a man in the audience.

"That man over there says that women need to be helped into carriages, and lifted over ditches, and to have the best places everywhere.... Nobody ever helped *me* into carriages, or over mud puddles, or give *me* any best place."

Sojourner reared back and thundered: "And aren't I a woman?"

The crowd, fickle as ever, murmured in approval.

"Look at me!" she commanded. "Look at my arm."

"I have plowed and planted and gathered into barns, and no man could head me—and aren't I a woman?"

The crowd began to come alive now, saying: "Yes. Yes."

"I have born'd five children and seen them most all sold off into slavery, and when I cried out with mother's grief, none but Jesus heard—*and aren't I a woman?*"

Over and over again, Sojourner repeated the rhythmic question, and the audience whooped and hollered with each repetition.

The great woman turned now and attacked another flank.

"Then that little man in black there, he says women can't have as much rights as man, 'cause Christ wasn't a woman"; Sojourner pulled herself to her full height and bounced the question off the wall. "Where did your Christ come from?"

The preacher sat silent, and Sojourner repeated the question, thunderously:

"Where did your Christ come from?"

She paused artfully, and then answered: "From God and a woman! Man had nothing to do with him."

Now that the enemy was vanquished, the white feminists came to their feet, waving delicate handkerchiefs and cheering. Sojourner Truth watched them for a moment, an ambivalent smile on her lips, and then she said quietly: "Obliged to ye for hearing on me; and now old Sojourner ain't got nothing more to say."

In this sally, one of the most brilliant improvisational thrusts in the history of American oratory, Sojourner's fundamental traits as a person emerged — passion, presence, and a wisdom that transcended books and schools. She was also filled with a latent sense of power. On one occasion, she said that she felt as though the "power of a nation was within [her]." This power stemmed from a mystical sense of the overwhelming presence and power of God. It was always Sunday with Sojourner and every place was a church.

Perhaps the best-known incident of her life underlined this sense of being always and everywhere in God's hand. The incident happened in Boston shortly before the Civil War. Sojourner was again lolling near the platform in a huge hall; again, men and women thought she was asleep. Frederick Douglass, the leading orator of the age, was on the platform detailing the horrors of the hour. The black abolitionist spoke with chilling eloquence of man's inhumanity to man, of the whippings and the croppings and the lynchings and the —

"Frederick" — the big booming voice electrified the crowd — "Frederick," Sojourner Truth asked, "is God dead?"

God was not dead, but, as always, he was helping those who helped themselves. With the help of Sojourner Truth and Frederick Douglass and other black and white abolitionists, God was soon "tramping out the vintage where the grapes of wrath are stored."

During the Civil War, Sojourner immersed herself in war work. She nursed Union soldiers and improved the sanitary facilities in the "contraband" camps. She also paid a celebrated call on Abraham Lincoln.

Washington at this point was an unmarked battlefield for black men and women. The major point of contention was the Jim Crow transit system. Sojourner Truth attacked this system frontally, staging a series of sit-ins on "white" horse-drawn street cars. Sojourner's sit-ins, however, were not particularly nonviolent. When the street cars stopped to pick up white passengers, Sojourner would barge in and dare the conductor to throw her off. One conductor accepted the challenge and roughed up the elderly black woman. Sojourner sued the company and won.

After the war, the old warrior bought a house in Battle Creek, Michigan, and settled down to a domestic life with her children and grandchildren. But she did not remain long in this domestic retreat. The white terror in the South and the disembowelling of the Reconstruction program galvanized her into action. She urged embattled blacks to come North where they could make a fight of it and asked Congress to allocate land and money for the establishment of black colonies in the Wild West. "America," she said, "owes my people some of the dividends. She can afford to pay, and she must pay. I shall make them understand that there is a debt to the Negro people which they never can repay. At least then, they must make amends."

By this time, Sojourner was in the winter of life. Many people believed she was well over a hundred, and Sojourner, always aware of the drama of her cause, did nothing to disabuse their awe-stricken faith.

Sojourner was, in fact, approaching ninety, and her body knew it. Though racked by excruciating pain from fever sores and varicose ulcers, she pressed her lonely and unpromising fight for a just Reconstruction. No one heeded her pleas and she went home to Battle Creek to await the end. She waited with hope and with a bright vision of the future. "These colored people," she said, "will bring the whites out of Egyptian darkness into marvelous light. The white people cannot do it, but these will.... The colored people are going to be *a* people. Do you think God has had them robbed and scourged all the days of their life for nothing!"

Sojourner had always said that death was not an end but a beginning. It was like walking, she said, from one room to another. On November 26, 1883, at three in the morning, Sojourner Truth, the American original, crossed the sill between the two rooms. "I ain't gonna die, honey," she had said. "I'se going home, like a shooting star."

GUERRILLA

in the

COTTONFIELDS

Harriet Tubman

She deserves to be placed first on the list of American heroines.

SAMUEL J. MAY

HARRIET TUBMAN

Black as the night, and as bold, she slipped across the Mason-Dixon line and headed for a rendezvous point in the old slave South. With revolver cocked, she moved unerringly across the fields and through the forests, flitting from tree to tree and from ditch to ditch.

From time to time, she froze in her tracks, forewarned by a personal radar that never failed. A broken twig, the neigh of a horse, a cough, a sneeze: these said danger ahead. And so she halted, listening, waiting, her body tensed for attack. She was a gentle woman, but she was black and she could ill afford sentimentality. There was a price on her head, some forty thousand dollars, and the slightest mistake would mean death. Slave patrols, guards, planters — eyes — were everywhere, and all were on the lookout for fugitive slaves in general and one woman in particular. No matter. The short black woman was without nerves and she had no peer, male or female, in her chosen trade: organizing and managing slave escapes. She had been this way many times before and she had brought out hundreds of slaves. Now she was at it again, slipping through Pennsylvania, Delaware, and Maryland.

On and on she went, deeper and deeper into the slave South, traveling by night and hiding by day, moving closer and closer to a rendezvous point on the Eastern Shore of Maryland near Cambridge. There, a group of slaves forewarned by a code letter to a sympathetic free Negro, waited with terror and with hope. Harriet Tubman materialized from nowhere, rapping her code on a chosen door in the slave quarters or standing deep in the woods and singing, for a tantalizing moment, a few bars of a Spiritual code:

I'll meet you in the morning
Safe in the Promised Land,
On the other side of Jordan,
Bound for the Promised Land.

Waiting ears, hearing the code knock or the code song, perked up and word raced through the cabins of the initiated: "Moses is here." After certain preparations, "the woman," as she was called, led a group of slaves through Maryland, Delaware, Pennsylvania, and New York into the Promised Land of Canada. Nineteen times she made this dangerous round trip; nineteen times, single-handed, she baited the collective might of the slave power — and nineteen times she won. What she did, Thomas Wentworth Higginson said, was "beyond anything in fiction." Sarah Bradford, her first biographer, said "her name deserves to be handed down to posterity, side by side with the names of Jeanne D'Arc, Grace Darling, and Florence Nightingale. . . ." In truth, her name should stand higher for, as Mrs. Bradford added, "not one of these women, noble and brave as they were, [showed] more courage, and power of endurance, in facing danger and death than the woman known to posterity as Harriet Tubman, 'the Moses of her people.'"

The great slave rebel, whose name struck terror in the hearts of Eastern Shore planters, was born a slave and lived the life of a slave. She was born in 1820 or 1821 in Bucktown near Cambridge on the Eastern Shore, one of the eleven children of Harriet Green and Benjamin Ross. As a child, she was called both Harriet and Araminta. But she was never really a child. For at the age of five, she was working full-time, cleaning white people's houses during the day and tending their babies at night. When she fell asleep, she was whipped mercilessly.

"I grew up," she said later, "like a neglected weed—ignorant of liberty, having no experience of it. I was not happy or contented: every time I saw a white man I was afraid of being carried away. I had two sisters carried away in a chain gang—one of them left two children. We were always uneasy. . . . I think slavery is the next thing to hell. If a person would send another into bondage he would, it appears to me, be bad enough to send him to hell if he could."

Harriet was a rebellious child. It would not be too much of an exaggeration to say that she was born a rebel. Fighting back with whatever she could lay hands on, she survived; and, having survived, she set her sights higher. By the time Harriet reached her teens, her master, despairing of ever making her a house servant, put her out to field where she plowed, drove oxen, and cut wood. She remembered later with pride that she "could lift huge barrels of produce and draw a loaded stone boat like an ox."

All this time, young Harriet was gathering fury against the slave system. She was, by all accounts, the despair of white overseers, who could not break her rebellious will. On one occasion, a male slave abandoned his post and went to town. The slave was closely followed by the overseer, who was closely followed by Harriet. The overseer cornered the slave in a store and called on Harriet for aid. The young slave girl, who was only thirteen, ignored the order and went to the aid of the slave. When the slave dashed through the door, Harriet stepped between him and the overseer. The overseer, enraged, picked up a two-pound weight and flung it at the escaping slave. The weight struck Harriet, tearing a hole in her skull.

For several weeks, Harriet hovered between life and death. Then, slowly, she began to recover. It was discovered later that the blow had pushed a portion of her skull against her brain. Ever afterwards, she suffered from what was called a "stupor" or "sleeping sickness." Four or five times a day, she would suddenly fall asleep. After a short spell, she would regain consciousness and continue the conversation or her work at the precise point where she left off. Because of this ailment, white people in the neighborhood, and some slaves, assumed that Harriet was "half-witted"—an assumption the wily Harriet encouraged.

During her lengthy convalescence, Harriet developed a deep and intensely personal religious faith. She had always been a dreamy, indrawn child. But now she gave herself over wholly to God, "praying," she said, "without ceasing." She prayed first for her master, asking God to soften his heart and make him mindful of the sacred ties between human beings. But the master did not change. Word reached Harriet one day that he was planning to sell her and other members of the family to the deep South. "Then," said Harriet, "I changed my prayer. I began to pray, 'Oh, Lord, if you aren't ever going to change that man's heart, kill him, Lord, and take him out of the way, so he won't do no more mischief.'" Later, on the death of her master, Harriet was smitten with a sense of contrition. "He died, just as he had lived," she said, "a wicked, bad man. Oh, then, it 'peared like I would give the world full of silver and gold if I had it, to bring that poor soul back. I would give *myself*; I would give everything! But he was gone, I couldn't pray for him no more."

Putting her master behind her, Harriet began now to consider seriously the possibilities of escape. The constantly recurring idea of escape struck such deep roots in her mind that she dreamed repeatedly of a "line" across which there was freedom and human dignity. After her marriage to John Tubman, a free black man, the dreams increased in frequency and intensity. When Harriet learned that her new master planned to sell her and two of her brothers, she decided to run away. She tried to persuade her brothers to accompany her, but they refused. So she set out alone in the summer of 1849, traveling at night through Maryland and Delaware and finally reaching Philadelphia. She went with a threat in her heart. "For," said she, "I had reasoned this out in my mind; there was one of two things I had a *right* to, liberty or death; if I could not have one, I would have the other, for no man should take me alive...."

When she crossed the "line" between slavery and freedom, she was overwhelmed by a sense of fulfillment. "I looked at my hands," she said, "to see if I was the same person now I was free. There was such a glory over everything, the sun came like gold through the trees, and over the fields...."

But there was a shadow in Harriet's Eden. She perceived suddenly with startling clarity that she could never be free until her people were free. "I knew of a man," she said, "who was sent to State Prison for twenty-five years. All these years he was always thinking of his home, and counting by years, months, and days, the time till he should be free, and see his family and friends once more. The years roll on, the time of imprisonment is over, the man is free. He leaves the prison gates, he makes his way to his old home, but his old home is not there. The house in which he had dwelt in his childhood had been torn down, and a new one had been put up in its place; his family were gone, their very name was forgotten, there was no one to take him by the hand to welcome him back to life."

"So it was with me," Harriet added. "I had crossed the line of which I had so long been dreaming. I was free; but there was no one to welcome me to the land of freedom. I was a stranger in a strange land, and my home after all was down in the old cabin quarter, with the old folks, and my brothers and sisters. But to this solemn resolution I came; I was free, and they should be free also; I would make a home for them in the North, and the Lord helping me, I would bring them all here...."

So resolving, Harriet Tubman dedicated herself to work unceasingly for the complete emancipation of her people. In Philadelphia and other Northern cities, she worked day and night as a domestic. When she had accumulated enough money to finance a slave escape, she would return to the South and lead out a group of slaves. The first trip occurred shortly after her escape. In December, 1850, she returned to Maryland and spirited out her sister and two children. Four months later, she returned and guided her brother and two other slaves to freedom. Returning to the South in the fall of 1851 for her husband, she discovered he had married again. This was a shattering blow, but Harriet had no time to grieve over personal problems. Abandoning her original plan, putting John Tubman behind her, she organized a group of slaves and carried them to Canada. Thereafter, she made a series of forays into the South, bringing out relatives, friends, and anyone else who wanted to go.

To understand what Harriet was about, to understand the magnitude of her accomplishments, it is necessary to understand the system she was challenging. The slave South was a totalitarian system. Every instrument of power in the South was bent to the detection and destruction of slaves like Harriet Tubman. To penetrate the defenses of this system, to guide hundreds of slaves of all ages and physical conditions through thousands of miles of closely guarded territory required tactical ability approaching genius.

Harriet approached her task with thoroughness and dispatch. Between trips, she accumulated money by working as a cook, maid, laborer. Since she could neither read nor write, she employed Northern confederates to write coded letters to free Negroes or sympathetic whites in the area she planned to visit. A free Negro in Cambridge, for example, received the following letter before a Harriet Tubman strike. "Read my letter to the old folks, and give my love to them, and *tell my brothers to be always watching unto prayer, and when the good old ship of Zion comes along, to be ready to step aboard.*" [Emphasis supplied.]

After contacting the slaves, Harriet accumulated the tools of her trade: a revolver and fresh ammunition, fake passes for slaves of varying description, and paregoric to drug babies. With these and other "tools" hidden on her person, she slipped across the Mason-Dixon line and made her way to selected plantations where slaves were informed of her presence by code songs, prayers, or some other stratagem. Selected slaves were then apprised of the rendezvous area and the time of departure. General Tubman, as she was called, was very strict about time. She waited for no one — not even a brother who was delayed on one trip by the imminent arrival of a new baby in his family.

Once the slaves were assembled, Harriet sized them up, searching them closely with her eyes. Satisfied, she placed the group under strict military discipline. During the trip, she was in absolute and total control and no one could question her orders. William Still, the black rebel who operated the key Philadelphia station of the Underground Railroad, said she "had a very short and pointed rule of law of her own which implied death to anyone who talked of giving out and going back." Once a slave committed himself to a Tubman escape, he was committed to freedom or death. On several occasions, slaves collapsed and said they were tired, sick, scared. Harriet always cocked her revolver and said: "You go on or die. Dead niggers tell no tales." Faced with a determined Harriet Tubman, slaves always found new strength and determination. During ten years of guerrilla action, the great commando leader never lost a slave through capture or return.

Of the tricks of her trade, Harriet was a past mistress. She almost always began her escapes on Saturday night. Since it was impossible to advertise for runaway slaves on Sunday, this gave her a twenty-four-hour start on pursuers. She also made a practice of escaping in the carriages of masters, covering the slaves with vegetables or baggage and driving all night Saturday and all day Sunday before abandoning the appropriated vehicle. This stratagem served two purposes. It rapidly moved escapees from the immediate neighborhood, and it befuddled guards and planters who assumed usually that a slave boldly driving a carriage was on an errand for his master.

After abandoning the carriage, Harriet and her charges made their way north by following the North Star or feeling the moss on the sides of trees. Harriet tried usually to keep her groups together, but she sometimes dispersed them, sending twos or threes through hostile towns. On occasions, she dressed men in women's clothes and vice versa.

In an emergency, the guerrilla leader acted swiftly, even ruthlessly. On one night, she escaped capture by hiding her charges in a manure pile and sticking straws in their mouths so they could breathe. On another trip, she eluded pursuers by buying tickets and putting the slaves on a train *heading south*. No one, of course, expected fugitive slaves to be on a southbound train.

The great slave rebel was helped enormously in her extraordinary career by a natural talent for acting. Indeed, Thomas Wentworth Higginson, the antislavery preacher, believed she was one of the greatest actresses and comediennes of the age. "One of her most masterly accomplishments," he said, "was the impression of a decrepit old woman. On one of her expeditions ... she had the incredible nerve to enter a village where lived one of her former masters. This was necessary for the carrying out of her plans for the trip. Her only disguise was a bodily assumption of age. To reinforce this, her subtle foresight prompted her to buy some live chickens, which she carried suspended by the legs from a cord. As she turned a corner she saw coming toward her none other than her old master. Lest he might see through her impersonation and to make an excuse for flight, she loosed the cord that held the fowls and, amid the laughter of the bystanders, gave chase to them as they flew squawking over a nearby fence."

No less effective was the use Harriet made of melody. She was proud of her singing voice and she used it repeatedly in managing slave escapes. Alice Stone Blackwell, the feminist leader, said: "If I remember correctly, Harriet Tubman told me that when she was convoying parties of fugitives, she used to guide them by the songs that she sang as she walked along the roads.... It was when her parties of fugitives were in hiding, that she directed them by her songs as to whether they might show themselves, or must continue to lie low.... No one would notice what was sung by an old colored woman, as she trudged along the road."

What made the Tubman exploits so extraordinary was the fact that she could not read or write. This led, on occasion, to hair-raising encounters. The story is told of the time she fell asleep on a train beneath a "wanted" poster bearing her likeness. Awakening and hearing several white men discussing her and the poster, Harriet grabbed a book and began to "read," praying fervently that she was not holding the book upside down. The white men lost interest for the poster said clearly that the "dangerous" wanted woman could neither read nor write.

A cool customer, Harriet Tubman — cool, determined and bold, never wanting for the right gesture or the right retort. Her steadiness stemmed from a total and absolute faith in God. She talked to God every day, believed He was always with her and would never let her down.

On one expedition, Harriet's personal radar told her there was danger, great danger, ahead. She discussed the matter with God, saying: "You been wid me in six troubles, Lord, be wid me in the seventh." What happened next was related by Thomas Garrett, who heard it from Harriet Tubman's lips. "She said that God told her to stop, which she did; and then asked him what she must do. He told her to leave the road, and turn to the left; she obeyed, and soon came to a small stream of tide-water; there was no boat; no bridge; she again inquired of her Guide what she was to do. She was told to go through. It was cold, in the month of March; but having confidence in her Guide, she went in; the water came up to her armpits; the men refused to follow till they saw her safe on the opposite shore. They then followed, and, if I mistake not, she had soon to wade a second stream, soon after which she came to a cabin of colored people, who took them all in, put them to bed, and dried their clothes, ready to proceed next night on the journey.... The strange part of the story we found to be, that the masters of these men had put up the previous day, at the railroad station near where she left, an advertisement offering a large reward for their apprehension."

From 1850 to December, 1860, the month of her last expedition, Harriet guided some three hundred slaves out of the South. Perhaps her most famous expedition occurred in 1857 when she returned for her father and mother. Learning that her father faced arrest and trial on a charge of aiding slaves to escape, she rushed to Maryland and "moved his case," she said, to "a higher court." At this point, Harriet's mother and father were old and decrepit. Neither could walk very fast. How then did Harriet Tubman succeed in moving them from Maryland to Canada? Thomas Garrett, who managed the Wilmington Underground Railroad station, said: "They started with an old horse, fitted out in primitive style with a straw collar, a pair of old chaise wheels, with a board on the axle to sit on, another board swung with ropes, fastened to the axle, to rest their feet on. She got her parents, who were both slaves belonging to different masters, on this rude vehicle to the railroad, put them in the cars, turned Jehu herself, and drove to town in a style that no human being ever did before or since." Harriet later moved her parents to Auburn, New York, where William H. Seward, one of her admirers, sold her a plot of land at a very reasonable price.

As a result of her underground work, the former slave became a heroine of the abolitionist crusade. During the late fifties, she began to appear on the platform as an antislavery and feminist advocate. "For eight or ten years previous to the breaking out of the Rebellion," William Wells Brown said, "all who frequented anti-slavery conventions, lectures, picnics, and fairs, could not fail to have seen a black woman of medium size, upper front teeth gone, smiling countenance, attired in coarse, but neat apparel, with an old-fashioned reticule or bag suspended by her side. . . ."

It was during this period that Harriet Tubman met John Brown, who said she was the "most of a man, naturally, that I ever met." Both John Brown and Harriet Tubman were rebels, if not revolutionaries, who were somewhat contemptuous of abolitionists who fought mainly with their voices and their pens. Because they shared the same vision of battle, the two rebels became close friends, and Harriet helped John Brown to plan his famous attack on Harpers Ferry. In fact, the evidence indicates that Harriet Tubman intended to accompany John Brown. But she became ill in October of 1859 and missed the celebrated raid. Thereafter, Harriet Tubman venerated John Brown over all other Americans, insisting that he was more responsible for the destruction of slavery than Abraham Lincoln. "It was not John Brown that died at Charlestown," she said. *"It was Christ;* — it was the Saviour of our people."

From the start, the slave rebel was cool toward Abraham Lincoln. She was critical of Lincoln's initial attempt to wage war without disturbing the institution of slavery. Recalling the old proverb, "Never wound a snake but kill it," she said the war could not be won until men addressed themselves to the root cause of the war — slavery. "God is ahead of Lincoln," she said. "God won't let Mister Lincoln beat the South till he does the right thing. Mister Lincoln, he is a great man, and I'm a poor Negro; but this Negro can tell Mister Lincoln how to save the money and the young men. He can do it by setting the Negroes free. Suppose there was an awfully big snake down there on the floor. He bites you. You send for the doctor to cut the bite; but the snake, he rolls up there, and while the doctor is doing it, he bites you again. The doctor cuts down that bite, but while he's doing it the snake springs up and bites you again, and so he keeps doing till you kill him. That's what Mister Lincoln ought to know."

During the first phase of the Civil War, Harriet Tubman continued her guerrilla strikes, leading slaves to federal lines in Maryland and other states. In May, 1862, she was sent by Governor Andrew of Massachusetts to Port Royal, South Carolina, which was then under the control of federal troops. She served in the Port Royal area as a liaison person between federal troops and freedmen and as a nurse in camp hospitals.

Even more important perhaps was her work as a Union Army spy, scout, and commando. At the request of Union officers, she organized an intelligence service, recruiting several former slaves from surrounding areas. She later accompanied Colonel James Montgomery on several raids in South Carolina and Georgia. Indeed, there is a great deal of evidence which indicates that Harriet, not Montgomery, was the commander of Montgomery's most famous exploit, the June 2, 1863, raid up South Carolina's Combahee River. Harriet's role in this raid was clearly indicated by a dispatch which appeared on the front page of the *Commonwealth*, a Boston newspaper, on July 10, 1863.

HARRIET TUBMAN

Col. Montgomery and his gallant band of 300 black soldiers, *under the guidance of a black woman*, dashed into the enemy's country, struck a bold and effective blow, destroying millions of dollars worth of commissary stores, cotton and lordly dwellings, and striking terror into the heart of rebeldom, brought off near 800 slaves and thousands of dollars worth of property, without losing a man or receiving a scratch. It was a glorious consummation.

After they were all fairly well disposed of in the Beaufort charge, they were addressed in strains of thrilling eloquence by their gallant deliverer, to which they responded in a song

"There is a white robe for thee,"

a song so appropriate and so heartfelt and cordial as to bring unbidden tears.

The Colonel was followed by a speech from the black woman, who led the raid, and under whose inspiration it was originated and conducted. For sound sense and real native eloquence, her address would do honor to any man, and it created a great sensation. . . .

Since the rebellion she has devoted herself to her great work of delivering the bondman, with an energy and sagacity that cannot be exceeded. *Many and many times she has penetrated the enemy's lines and discovered their situation and condition, and escaped without injury, but not without extreme hazard.* [Emphasis supplied.]

A few months later, Harriet helped to bury the dead and to nurse the wounded after the famous charge of the 54th Massachusetts Volunteers, an all-Negro regiment, on Fort Wagner in the Charleston, South Carolina, harbor. Her incisive description of the war, quoted later by Albert Bushnell Hart, probably referred to that battle. "And then we saw the lightning," she said, "and that was the guns; and then we heard the thunder, and that was the big guns; and then we heard the rain falling, and that was the drops of blood falling; and when we came to get in the crops, it was dead men that we reaped."

At war's end, Harriet returned to her home in Auburn and began a thirty-seven-year effort to get government compensation for three years of war services. She wanted the money not for herself but to found schools and rest homes for the freedmen and their children. Although high-ranking officers and officials furnished depositions and affidavits on her war services, the federal government never fully paid the claim.

It was, in part, to buttress Harriet's claims that Sarah H. Bradford wrote a book on her life in 1886. Harriet and the author requested commendations from several prominent Americans, including Frederick Douglass, who answered: "You ask for what you do not need when you call upon me for a word of commendation. I need such words from you more than you can need them from me, especially where your superior labors and devotions to the cause of the lately enslaved of our land are known as I know them. The difference between us is very marked. Most that I have done and suffered in the service of our cause has been in public, and I have received encouragement at every step of the way. You, on the other hand, have labored in a private way. I have wrought in the day—you in the night. I have had the applause of the crowd and the satisfaction that comes of being approved by the multitude, while the most that you have done has been witnessed by a few trembling, scared, and foot-sore bondsmen and women, whom you have led out of the house of bondage, and whose heartfelt '*God bless you*' has been your only reward. The midnight sky and the silent stars have been the witnesses of your devotion to freedom and of your heroism. Excepting John Brown—of sacred memory—I know of no one who has willingly encountered more perils and hardships to serve our enslaved people than you have. Much that you have done would seem improbable to those who do not know you as I know you...."

The book Douglass commended brought Harriet Tubman a thousand dollars which she contributed to black schools in the South. Harriet also maintained open house in her home in Auburn, giving all she had to the poor, the needy, and the infirm.

During this period, she married a young Union Army veteran she had met in the Port Royal area. Her new husband, Nelson Davis, was in poor health and he soon died. After his death, the government gave Harriet a widow's pension of eight dollars a month. The pension was later increased to twenty dollars a month.

By this time, Harriet Tubman was something of a legend to Americans. She was good copy for most newspapers, and reporters from all over the country came to Auburn to interview her. To Frank C. Drake of the *New York Herald*, she told a story that reflected rather accurately the vicissitudes of her life:

"You wouldn't think that after I served the flag so faithfully I should come to want in its folds."

She looked musingly toward a nearby orchard, and she asked suddenly:

"Do you like apples?"
On being assured that I did, she said:
"Did you ever plant an apple tree?"
With shame I confessed I had not.
"No," she said, "but somebody else planted them. I liked apples when I was young, and I said, 'Some day I'll plant apples myself for other young folks to eat,' and I guess I did it."

Frank C. Drake noted in his dispatch that Harriet Tubman told this story "not plaintively, but rather with a flash of scorn in her eyes." At the time of this interview, Harriet was in need. But she was referring here to a deeper, trans-personal need. It grieved her that the government for which she fought had turned its back on her. And she was deeply concerned about the atrocities in the South. More than once, in this period, the tough old woman wept for the ingratitude of man.

As the years passed, turning the fork of the fateful twentieth century, Harriet Tubman girded herself for one last effort on behalf of her lifelong dream, a "John Brown Home" for indigent black people. By peddling fruit and by begging, she accumulated enough money to buy land and lay the foundations for the home. She later deeded the property and her home to the African Methodist Episcopal Zion Church.

As 1913 approached, Harriet turned her face toward the other world. She went to her favorite AME Zion Church for the last time and told the parishioners that the end was near. "I am nearing the end of my journey," she said. "I can hear them bells a-ringing, I can hear the angels singing, I can see the hosts a-marching. I hear somebody say: 'There is one crown left and that is for Old Aunt Harriet and she shall not lose her reward.'"

On March 10, 1913, in the fiftieth year of Emancipation, Harriet Tubman claimed her crown. She was buried with military rites and the next year the city of Auburn closed down in an unprecedented one-day memorial to the rebel and Union spy. The *Auburn Citizen*, as Earl Conrad noted, caught the spirit and meaning of this occasion in an editorial.

> The meeting at the Auditorium last night may be said to rank among the most unique in the history of this state, if not the nation. Every thoughtful person in the audience carried away the thought — what a remarkable woman Harriet Tubman must have been to deserve this tribute, an enduring monument from the white race to one of the lowliest and most humble of the blacks! Where has anything like it been recorded! ...
>
> How many of the white race exist today who will ever merit equal recognition with Harriet Tubman?

NAY-SAYER
of the
BLACK REVOLT

Henry Highland Garnet

> *The diabolical injustice by which*
> *your liberties are cloven down,*
> NEITHER GOD NOR ANGELS, OR
> JUST MEN, COMMAND YOU TO
> SUFFER FOR A SINGLE MOMENT.
> THEREFORE, IT IS YOUR SOLEMN
> AND IMPERATIVE DUTY TO USE
> EVERY MEANS, BOTH MORAL,
> INTELLECTUAL, AND PHYSICAL,
> THAT PROMISES SUCCESS.
>
> **HENRY HIGHLAND GARNET,**
> **ADDRESS TO SLAVES**

HENRY HIGHLAND GARNET

H ENRY HIGHLAND GARNET was perhaps the greatest nay-sayer in the history of black protest.

Refusing to accept oppression, saying "No!" loud and often and backing it up with the flesh and blood of deeds, Garnet sculptured a testament of defiance that affirmed not only the black man but the community of man. As the radical forerunner of Frederick Douglass, he held up a banner of uncompromising resistance. Man's freedom, he declared, consisted in the simple and pulverizing power to say *No*. Men who refused to make that gesture, he added, sinned against God by making themselves co-authors of their own degradation.

Teacher, preacher, editor, apostle of revolt and a general strike, Henry Highland Garnet told his contemporaries a truth so bitter that they paid him the compliment of fleeing in horror from his vision.

The vision that informed Garnet's life was a product of a supremely personal sense of history. Born December 23, 1815 in New Market, Maryland, Garnet was the scion of a long line of African warriors and rulers. His grandfather was a ruler of the Mandingo tribe, and his father, George, kept the old fire burning in an American setting. As a child, Garnet teethed on the grandeur of ancient Africa and developed an almost religious faith in the mission and destiny of Afro-Americans. His father fired this faith by an audacious act of affirmation. Securing permission to attend the funeral of a slave on a distant plantation, he managed to escape with his wife, daughter, and young Henry, who was then nine. The Garnets made their way to New York City, where Henry attended the Free African schools as a classmate of Ira Aldridge and Alexander Crummell.

Because of the poverty of his family, Garnet dropped out of school to earn money as a hand on sailing vessels. Returning home one day in 1829, the future leader came face to face with racial reality. In his absence, slavecatchers — who roamed the streets of New York City in those days — had scattered his family. Worse, they had captured his beloved sister. On that day, Henry Highland Garnet the revolutionary was born. Vowing vengeance, he bought a large clasp knife, opened it in his pocket and walked slowly down Broadway, hoping that a slavecatcher would seize him. Family friends, fearful for his safety and his sanity, interceded and sent him to Long Island, where he worked for two years as an indentured servant. During this interlude Garnet's right leg was injured and he afterwards suffered a strange malady appropriately named "white swelling." The leg was later amputated.

Although he was in almost constant pain, Garnet returned to New York City and resumed his education. Later, in 1835, he was one of a handful of black students who integrated Noyes Academy in Canaan, New Hampshire. The presence of Garnet and other black students infuriated the Puritans of Canaan, who declared the academy a public nuisance. After a bitter campaign of vituperation, three hundred citizens, aided by one hundred oxen, attached ropes to the school and dragged it to a swamp. Then, hooting and howling, they surrounded the home in which the black students were barricaded. Garnet, who was a born leader of men, rallied the rattled students and set them to work moulding bullets. Lame, suffering from a fever, and leaning on a crutch, the courageous young man organized a defense that probably saved the students' lives. Alexander

Crummell, who later became a famous Episcopalian priest, left an eyewitness account of the confrontation:

"About eleven o'clock," he said, "the tramp of horses was heard approaching; and as one rapid rider passed the house he fired at it. Garnet quickly replied to it by a discharge of a double barrelled shotgun which blazed away through the window. At once the hills for many a mile around reverberated with the sound. Lights were seen from scores of houses on every side of the town, and villages far and near were in a state of great excitement. But the musket shot by Garnet doubtless saved our lives. The cowardly ruffians dared not attack us. Notice, however, was given to us to quit the State within a fortnight. When we left, the Canaan mob assembled on the outskirts of the village and fired field-pieces charged with powder at our wagon."

Undaunted by the Canaan catastrophe, Garnet, Crummell, and the other black students entered Oneida Institute at Whitesboro, New York. In 1840, Garnet was graduated at the top of his class. Settling in Troy, New York, he taught school and studied theology for two years. In 1842 he was ordained as a minister and installed as pastor of the Liberty Street Presbyterian Church.

By this time, Garnet was in the advance guard of the fight for black liberation. In 1840, while still a student, he had attracted national attention with a slashing attack on slavery at the annual convention of the American Antislavery Society. Now, with a base of operations, he branched out, operating an Underground Railroad station in Troy and editing the *Clarion* and other pioneer black newspapers.

The antislavery crusade at this juncture was in a transitional phase of diffuse groping. Frederick Douglass had not made his appearance as an independent actor and the props and machinery were in the hands of abolitionists pursuing a policy of passive resistance. The abolitionists were making large contributions via the Underground Railroad, but the movement as a whole suffered from an inability of leaders to define and articulate programs of resistance for the slaves themselves. Indeed, it was considered bad form to make a direct appeal to the slaves. Some abolitionists, moreover, viewed black leaders as members of the supporting cast and arrogated to themselves the privileges of defining the antislavery posture.

Garnet, who rejected passive resistance as a policy of liberation, had nothing but scorn for the dominant drift of the movement. Black men, he said, could not be freed by agents; nor, he added significantly, could they be freed by white friends, however sincere or sacrificial. Taking a stance on the left of the movement, rejecting both paternalism and gradualism, Garnet reasserted the black man's role as an architect of his own destiny. With other black leaders, he revived the Negro Convention movement. He also called for a policy of open rebellion, moving to a radical position that frightened some of the most radical of the white abolitionists.

At the 1843 Negro convention, Garnet startled America with what was probably the most brilliant idea of the whole antislavery campaign — a general slave strike. He was only twenty-eight — tall, thin, black — when he limped, favoring his wooden leg, to the platform in Buffalo, New York. For a moment on that hot August day, Garnet was silent, holding the black delegates from ten states with piercing eyes that seemed, William Wells Brown said, "to look through you." Then, in a deep, vibrant voice, he began, speaking not to the delegates but directly to the slaves.

"Your brethren of the North, East, and West," he said with barely concealed contempt, "have been accustomed to meet together in National Conventions, to sympathize with each other, and to weep over your unhappy conditions. In these meetings we have addressed all classes of the free, but we have never until this time, sent a word of consolation and advice to you. We have been contented in sitting still and mourning over your sorrows, earnestly hoping that before this day your sacred liberty would have been restored. But we have hoped in vain. Years have rolled on, and tens of thousands have been borne on streams of blood and tears, to the shores of eternity."

It was time, Garnet said, to stop "sitting still" and "hoping" and "sympathizing." With sharp, stinging jabs, he recounted "the dark catalogue of this nation's sins."

"Nearly three millions of your fellow-citizens are prohibited by law and public opinion . . . from reading the Book of Life. Your intellect has been destroyed as much as possible. . . . The oppressors themselves have become involved in your ruin. They have become weak, sensual, and rapacious — they have cursed you — they have cursed themselves — they have cursed the earth which they have trod."

Warming to his subject, thinking perhaps of his sister, of his mother, of "the millions [who] have come from eternity into time and have returned again to the world of spirits," Garnet told the slaves that resistance was a religious duty. "Your condition does not absolve you from your moral obligation. The diabolical injustice by which your liberties are cloven down, NEITHER GOD, NOR ANGELS, OR JUST MEN, COMMAND YOU TO SUFFER FOR A SINGLE MOMENT. THEREFORE IT IS YOUR SOLEMN AND IMPERATIVE DUTY TO USE EVERY MEANS, BOTH MORAL, INTELLECTUAL, AND PHYSICAL, THAT PROMISE SUCCESS."

What did Garnet recommend?

"Brethren," he said, "the time has come when you must act for yourselves. . . . Look around you, and behold the bosoms of your loving wives heaving with untold agonies! Hear the cries of your poor children! Remember the stripes your fathers bore. Think of the torture and disgrace of your noble mothers. Think of your wretched sisters, loving virtue and purity, as they are driven into concubinage and are exposed to the unbridled lusts of incarnate devils. Think of the undying glory that hangs around the ancient name of Africa—and forget not that you are native born American citizens, and as such, you are justly entitled to all the rights that are granted to the freest. Think how many tears you have poured out upon the soil which you have cultivated with unrequited toil and enriched with your blood; and then go to your lordly enslavers and tell them plainly that you are *determined to be free....* Do this, and *forever after cease to toil for the heartless tyrants*, who give you no other reward but stripes and abuses. If they then commence the work of death, they, not you, will be responsible for the consequences. You had better all die—*die immediately*, than live slaves and entail your wretchedness upon your posterity. If you would be free in this generation, here is your only hope. However much you and all of us may desire it, there is not much hope of redemption without the shedding of blood. If you must bleed, let it all come at once—*rather die free men, than live to be slaves.*

Garnet returned to this theme several times, holding up the examples of Nat Turner, Denmark Vesey, and other slave rebels. Then, in a thunderous peroration, he shouted:

"Brethren, arise, arise! Strike for your lives and liberties. Now is the day and the hour.... In the name of God, we ask, are you men? Where is the blood of your fathers? Has it all run out of your veins? Awake, awake; millions of voices are calling you! Your dead fathers speak to you from their graves. Heaven, as with a voice of thunder, calls on you to arise from the dust....

"Let your motto be resistance! *resistance!* RESISTANCE!"

When Garnet was done, the hall heaved in applause. A white reporter said Garnet had the crowd laughing, shouting and weeping at his will. The reporter added that "for one hour of his life his [the reporter's] mind had not been [his] own, but wholly at the control of the eloquent Negro."

After the shouting had died down, some of the delegates had sober second thoughts. Frederick Douglass, then under the sway of the Garrison doctrine of passive resistance, opposed adoption of the speech, saying there was "too much physical force" in Garnet's words and bearing. After a heated debate, the delegates declined to endorse Garnet's appeal by the slim margin of one vote. But Garnet had the last word. By 1848, most abolitionists had moved to his position, and his address was printed and circulated by black conventions and by John Brown.

Garnet's fiery appeal for a general strike and slave revolt frightened many abolitionists. Maria W. Chapman, a Garrison disciple, attacked Garnet in the *Liberator* and urged black people to reject the voice of radicalism and despair. Garnet replied immediately. "I was born in slavery," he wrote in a personal letter, "and have escaped to tell you and others what the monster has done, and is still doing. It, therefore, astonishes me to think that you should desire to sink me again to the condition of a *slave*, by forcing me to think as you do. My crime is, that I have dared to think, and act, contrary to your opinion.... If it has come to this, that I must think and act as you do, because you are an abolitionist or be exterminated by your thunder, then I do not hesitate to say that your abolitionism is abject slavery." Mrs. Chapman had suggested, by implication anyway, that Garnet was being led astray by misguided white men. Garnet was enraged. "You are not the only person who has told your humble servant that his humble productions have been produced by the 'counsel' of some Anglo-Saxon.... I can think on the subject of human rights without 'counsel' either from the men of the West or"—he added acidly—"the women of the East."

Garnet went his lonely way, taking advanced positions and breaking new ground for the movement. An ardent advocate of radical political action, he participated in the founding of the Liberty party, which led by various mutations to the Republican party. At the party convention in 1843, Garnet and Charles B. Ray, a black abolitionist and editor, were elected to official positions, becoming the first black men to take an active part in the deliberations of a national political convention. The famous reformer also found time to champion temperance and education. Considered by many to be one of the finest preachers of his age, he crisscrossed the country, lecturing and preaching to large audiences.

The dominant motifs of Garnet's public life — largeness of spirit, audacity, total commitment — informed his relations with his friends and members of his family. In 1842, he married Julia Williams, a former classmate; and their home was a haven for the avant garde of the antislavery movement. His great friend, Alexander Crummell, said: "There are two words, which, I think, more than any other will serve to delineate his character — LARGENESS and SWEETNESS.... Things, ideas of magnitude, grand prospects, seemed ever, even in boyhood, to occupy his mind."

After passage of the fugitive slave bill of 1850, Garnet spent three busy years in Europe, lecturing on slavery in English and fluent French and German. He served for a brief time as a missionary in Jamaica, returning to America in 1855 to become pastor of Shiloh Presbyterian Church in New York City.

By this time, the antislavery movement had caught up with Garnet and he threw himself, with renewed vigor, into the fight. As an underground worker, employed by various vigilance committees, he played an active part in several guerrilla actions against the fugitive slave bill. John Brown, who admired his courage, conferred with him on the plans for the Harpers Ferry assault.

Throughout this period, there was a continuing dialogue between Douglass and Garnet. Between these two titans, the major black actors in the antislavery drama, no love was lost. Usually, in this period, Garnet could be found on the opposite side of any issue Douglass raised, and vice versa. Garnet scored Douglass' coolness toward organized religion, and Douglass scored Garnet's penchant for black nationalism and his plans for organizing an African Colonization Society. After Douglass abandoned the Garrisonian program, the two men were not divided on substantive matters. But the clash continued, to the detriment of a unified black front. Worse, white men were able to pit Douglass against Garnet, thereby diminishing the force of both. As the Civil War approached, this intramural squabble, which was basically a personal and sometimes petty contest between two independent and strong-willed men, receded in importance and all segments of the black community joined forces for the final push toward black liberation.

Having played a major role in sowing the seeds of black emancipation, Garnet saw the Civil War as a time of harvest. Accepting the pulpit of the fashionable Fifteenth Street Presbyterian Church in the nation's capital, he agitated for the abolition of slavery and the employment of slaves as soldiers in the Union Army. Despite his disabilities, he recruited black soldiers and served as chaplain for a regiment of black troops. Republican leaders recognized his key role by designating him speaker for the anniversary celebration of the Emancipation Proclamation. Garnet delivered the "Memorial Discourse" on February 12, 1865, in the House of Representatives, thereby becoming the first black man to speak in the halls of Congress. When Lincoln was assassinated, his widow presented two of his canes to Garnet and Douglass, the two major black leaders.

After the war, Garnet returned to New York City and Shiloh Presbyterian Church. He continued to champion unpopular causes, speaking out against the counterrevolution in the South and organizing a committee to agitate for Cuban independence. Appointed minister resident to Liberia in 1881, Garnet prepared for what he considered one of the major events of his life—the return to the land of his fathers as a representative of the free men of the New World. Going by way of England, he arrived in Liberia on December 28, 1881, and fell ill almost immediately. Two months later he was dead. They buried him, Crummell said, "like a prince, this princely man, with the blood of a long line of chieftains in his veins, in the soil of his fathers. The entire military forces of the capital of the republic turned out to render a last tribute of respect and honor. The President and his cabinet, the ministers of every name, the president, professors and students of the college . . . as well as the townsmen, attended his obsequies as mourners. . . . Minute guns were fired at every footfall of his procession. And when they laid him lowly in the sod, there was heard on the hills, in the valleys and on the waters, the tributary peal of instantaneous thunder which announced through the still air the closing of the grave. There he lies, the deep Atlantic but a few steps beyond, as perpetual surges beat at his very feet, chanting ever more the deep anthems of the ocean, the solemn requiem of the dead."

GOD'S ANGRY MAN

John Brown

I would sing how an old man, tall, with white hair,
*   mounted the scaffold in Virginia*
(I was at hand, silent I stood with teeth shut close, I watch'd,
I stood very near you old man when cool and indifferent,
but trembling with age and your unheal'd wounds
*   you mounted the scaffold).*

WALT WHITMAN

JOHN BROWN

SOMETHING IN the face, something in the eyes—
something threatening, something equivocal, *something terrible*—
set him apart from other men.

Passing him in the streets, strangers turned for another look.
Talking to him in a room, friends recoiled in anxiety from the
raging fire of "the most alarming eyes in American history."

Some men said he was mad.

Some men said he was a fool.

But some men said he was a saint.

Abraham Lincoln called him a misguided fanatic. Jefferson
Davis called him a bloodthirsty murderer, but Ralph Waldo
Emerson and Harriet Tubman and Henry David Thoreau said
he was a nineteenth-century Christ.

Fool or fanatic, madman or prophet, devil or saint: with such
words friends and foes tried to capture the transcendent spirit
of John Brown, a terrible-visaged old white man who believed
he was ordained by God to suffer and to die for the freedom of
the black man.

Indifferent both to praise and blame, possessed by the idea
that he had "a letter of marque from God" to destroy slavery by
whatever means necessary, blind to color, scornful of status and
contemptuous of reformers who fought only with words, John
Brown made himself the most controversial figure in American
history by saying in action that "to recognize an evil and not to

strike it" was the highest evil. "Talk! Talk! Talk!" he said derisively of black and white reformers, adding that "whenever there is a right to be done, there is a 'thus saith the Lord' that it shall be done."

So believing, so saying, John Brown hurled himself with a bloody sprawl against the organized power of slavery in a desperate attempt to wrench history out of its orbit. With God and twenty-one men, five blacks and sixteen whites, he invaded the state of Virginia, captured the town of Harpers Ferry, seized the U.S. arsenal, and freed some fifty slaves. Defeated finally, captured and caged, he bedazzled America with a demonstration of faith and fortitude that melted the hearts of enemies and friends. Then, sure that death would serve his cause, he went, cool and indifferent, to the gallows. With this series of acts, John Brown shattered the dam of words that held back the turbulent emotions behind the words "slave" and "Negro." With this series of acts, he created, almost singlehanded, the inflamed emotional climate that led to a Civil War.

More than any other individual, John Brown was responsible for forcing the issue of black liberation. More than any other white man, this old man was consumed, literally consumed, by the idea of black liberation. "His zeal in the cause of freedom," Frederick Douglass said, "was infinitely superior to mine. Mine was as the taper light; his was the burning sun. Mine was bounded by time; his stretched away to the silent shores of eternity. I could speak for the slave; John Brown could fight for the slave. I could live for the slave; John Brown could die for the slave."

How explain this?

How explain a man who was willing to give for black people what some black people were not willing to give for themselves?

How explain a man who was a pacifist at twenty, a hardheaded businessman at forty, a terrorist at fifty-six, and a revolutionary at fifty-nine?

The answer, of course, is that the man cannot be explained except by reference to the totality of his life. Behind John Brown's indignation lay a long and relevant experience. In fact, it can be said that his whole life before 1859 was, in a sense, a gestation period for the birth he gave to himself in the fire and fury of Harpers Ferry.

The road to Harpers Ferry began far to the north in Torrington, Connecticut, where John Brown was born on May 9, 1800, to Owen Brown, "a poor but respectable farmer," and Ruth Mills Brown. As a child, John Brown was steeled in what he called the "school of adversity." From the beginning, the young boy was embroiled in a never-ending struggle with nature and with man's fate. The Puritan world into which he was born and by which he was moulded was a world of struggle with and against God, the flesh, and the devil. Early, John Brown went to the fields, driving cattle, tending sheep, doing the work of a man in a man's world; even earlier, before he could understand its meaning, he came to know the deeply rooted shadows of the Puritan soul. When he was five, the family moved to Hudson, Ohio, then one of the most remote areas in America. There, under the omnipresent shadow of the red man, John Brown spent his formative years, tramping barefoot in "buckskin breeches" across the fields and forests, spending as much time "as was consistent with good manners" in the Indian settlements. There, also, John Brown came under the influence of the black man, watching, wide-eyed and with beating heart, as his father, an ardent abolitionist, slipped black slaves through the community on the Underground Railroad. Through the red man, and the black, the future rebel experienced the tragic and titanic split in the Puritan psyche. And he took upon himself in a uniquely personal and uniquely terrible way the sins and guilt of his people.

He was barely twelve when the cause, his cause, seized him. By that time, he was mature beyond his years. So steady of eye and nerve was he that his father habitually entrusted him with the demanding job of driving cattle hundreds of miles to market. On one of these trips, the twelve-year-old boy stayed for a spell at the home of a businessman who owned a young slave who was "very active, intelligent, & good feeling." Young John Brown and the slave became friends, but the slave's master seized every opportunity to emphasize the differences in their statuses. John Brown said later that the man "made a great pet" of him, "brought him to table with his first company; & friends; called their attention to every little smart thing he said or did; & to the fact of his being more than a hundred miles from home with a company of cattle alone; while the Negro boy (who was fully if not more than his equal) was badly clothed, poorly fed; & lodged in cold weather; & beaten before his eyes with Iron Shovels or any other thing that came first to hand." Looking, listening, weighing, John Brown began to reflect on the "wretched, hopeless condition, of fatherless and motherless slave children. . . ." And he asked himself: "Is God their father?" There could be only one answer to that question for the intense, Bible-oriented son of Owen Brown; and Owen Brown's son did not shrink from the implications of that answer. John Brown said later that he immediately became "a most determined abolitionist" and swore "Eternal war on slavery."

John Brown the boy prefigured John Brown the revolutionary in more ways than one. Even as a child, he demonstrated unusual interest in the Bible; and although he was an indifferent student who spent very little time in school, he read the Bible, especially the Old Testament, with a vengeance. And with him, reading and knowing were roads to doing. One of the keys to his later life is the fact that he decided quite early that he was going to be a Christian in this world. At one point, he entered a college in Plainfield, Massachusetts, to prepare for the ministry. But an inflammation of the eyes forced him to give up that ambition.

This was the first in a series of extraordinary "failures" that led step by step to his ultimate triumph. Resigning himself to his fate, accepting, as he put it, God's will, he returned home and began working in his father's tannery. Not long after that he married Dianthe Lusk, the plain, pious daughter of a local widow. Six years later, in 1826, the young couple moved to Randolph (now New Richmond), Pennsylvania, with their children.

With his first marriage, the metamorphosis of John Brown began. He was at that point a prime example of the Puritan pioneer. Thin, spare, dour, "built for times of trouble," he presented a picture of single-minded determination. There was something categorical, something demanding, in the posture of this grim-mouthed young man; and then and later men found it easier to obey him than to refuse him.

In his personal habits, Brown was abstemious, even severe, regarding butter as a luxury of a frivolous civilization. At the sparsely furnished Brown home, days began and ended with prayer, and Sunday was a day of total and complete concentration on the affairs of the Lord. In the family circle, Brown was, by all accounts, stern and dictatorial. (He had, in all, twenty children, only eight of whom lived to maturity.) As Du Bois observed, his word was not only law but wish to members of his family. Though he was habitually stern, dominating his children by will power and a generous use of straps, he also possessed a paradoxical streak of feminine gentleness. It was he who walked the floor at night with sick children. It was he who nursed his wife night and day during bouts of illness.

John Brown's personal qualities made him a community leader in Randolph, where he cleared twenty-five acres of land, built a tannery and a barn, which had a cleverly concealed room for the use of fugitive slaves. Brown also took the lead in organizing a church, a school, and post-office. By 1831, he was a successful cattle breeder who employed as many as fifteen men in his tannery.

The young businessman moved now by successive phases, and successive failures, to what he called the "greatest or principal object" of his life—the destruction of slavery. In 1831, his first wife died a few hours after the death of a newly born infant. He remarried in 1832 and moved, in 1835, to Franklin Mills (now Kent), Ohio. There now followed a series of crushing blows that would have destroyed a lesser man. The depression of 1837 wiped him out financially. Five years later, in 1842, he was forced into bankruptcy. The next year, in September, four of his children died within a single week in a dysentery epidemic.

Like some modern Job, John Brown stumbled in the forties from disaster to disaster. How did he respond to these years of trial and tribulation? What did he do? What did he say? John Brown said the Lord had given and the Lord had taken away. "Blessed," he said in a letter of condolence to a member of his family—"Blessed be his great and holy name forever."

In the seven-year period between 1837 and 1844, John Brown tried hard to recoup his fortunes. He tanned hides, bred race horses, raised sheep, bought and sold cattle. Then, from 1844 to 1851, he was a wool merchant, operating from Akron, Ohio, and Springfield, Massachusetts. When this venture collapsed in 1854, John Brown turned his back on the business world with what seemed to be real relief.

Throughout the preceding years of business crises, John Brown the man had been struggling with John Brown the revolutionary. It can be said in fact that John Brown's repeated business reverses were reflections of the fact that John Brown's real business was not business. It is not possible to say with precision how long John Brown had known this. But there are indications that the idea that crowned his life possessed him in the early thirties and grew until it blotted out all other interests and considerations. Even as a businessman, he went out of his way to champion the cause of black people, hiding fugitive slaves in his warehouses and in his various homes, alienating friends and customers by his bare-boned attacks on bigotry in the church and other centers of power. Wherever he went, wherever he stopped, he sought out black people, visited their homes and invited them to his home. When, in 1839, a black minister named Fayette visited his home in Franklin, Ohio, he used the occasion to bind members of his family in a blood oath against slavery. John Brown Jr. recalled that his father first emphasized "his determination to make war on slavery.... He asked who of us were willing to make common cause with him in doing all in our power to 'break the jaws of the wicked and pluck the spoil out of his teeth,' naming each of us in succession, Are you, Mary, John, Jason, and Owen?"

Receiving affirmative answers from each member of his family, John Brown and Rev. Fayette, the black preacher, knelt on the floor and gave a sacred oath to God. "After prayer," John Brown Jr. continued, "[father] asked us to raise our right hands, and he then administered to us an oath, the exact terms of which I cannot recall, but in substance it bound us to secrecy and devotion to the purpose of fighting slavery by force and arms to the extent of our ability."

As the years wore on, John Brown's understanding of his mission widened and deepened. In the 1840's, during a protracted stay in Springfield, Massachusetts, he branched out as a counselor and advisor of radical black leaders. By that time, John Brown was in reality two men: the respectable merchant who moved on the fringes of the power structure, and the burgeoning revolutionary who urged black people to trust in God and keep their powder dry.

Gradually, under the impact of events, the revolutionary pushed the businessman into the shade. As a young man, John Brown had practiced pacifism and had refused to bear arms in war or peace. Now he became convinced that it was necessary to use the tools of the strong in order to protect the weak. He pressed this point on every black leader he could find, telling them that moral suasion would never end slavery and that speeches and pretty words were worse than useless.

Black leaders like Henry Highland Garnet and J. W. Loguen heeded John Brown's words because they perceived in him a kindred spirit. Brown possessed that rare gift of complete and total emphathy. He did not approach black people as a sympathetic outsider; he approached them as a man who shared and participated in their suffering. "I have talked with many men," Frederick Douglass said, "but I remember none, who seemed so deeply excited upon the subject of slavery as he. He would walk the room in agitation at the mention of the word."

It was this quality of experienced anguish that made John Brown a favorite with Douglass and other black leaders. When Douglass met Brown for the first time in 1847, the white rebel had already set his face toward the New Jerusalem which burned in his mind. "He was not averse," Douglass reported, "to the shedding of blood, and thought the practice of carrying arms would be a good one for the colored people to adopt, as it would give them a sense of manhood. No people, he said, could have self-respect or be respected who would not fight for their freedom. . . ."

It would appear from Douglass' account that the main outlines of the Harpers Ferry Raid were firm in Brown's mind at least twelve years before the fact. He was not yet free, however, to give the plan his full attention, for he was still a highly respected member of the business community. But in his spare time he continued to push toward his goal. Events in the outer world reinforced his determination. Year by year, the slave power continued to improve its position and its strength in the national government. A dramatic indication of this fact was the passage in 1850 of a fugitive slave bill which imperiled the lives and liberty of all black Americans.

Casting caution aside, Brown now made his first practical step on the road to Harpers Ferry. In 1851, four years after the

Douglass visit, he organized the League of Gileadites, a semi-military cadre, among the free black people of Springfield, Massachusetts. The "Agreement" of the organization, which was drawn up by John Brown, bound members to "provide [themselves] at once with suitable implements and [to] aid those who do not possess the means, if any such are disposed to join us." According to the "Agreement," the duty "of the aged, infirm, and young members of the League shall be to give instant notice to all members in case of an attack upon any of our people." John Brown himself added a word of advice. "Nothing," he said, "so charms the American people as personal bravery. . . . The trial for life of one bold and to some extent successful man, for defending his rights in good earnest, would arouse more sympathy throughout the nation than the accumulated wrongs and sufferings of more than three millions of our submissive colored population."

With the collapse of his last business venture in 1854, John Brown was free to give his every waking hour to his rapidly expanding plans for "close-quarter" resistance to slavery. Moving his family to North Elba, New York, he cut all ties to the business world and moved out into the deeps as a full-time rebel. At that precise moment, the passage of the Kansas-Nebraska Bill gave him an instrument which he used to project himself into the national spotlight. This bill provided that the Kansas territory would enter the union as a slave or free state depending on the votes of the citizens of the territory. What this meant as a practical matter was that the prize would go to the side that could mass the strongest force in the shortest amount of time. Since both antislavery and pro-slavery forces considered Kansas essential to the ultimate triumph of their cause, both sides rushed men and arms to the territory in an effort to gain leverage for the forthcoming struggle at the polls.

As the struggle widened, with a revolting series of assassinations, sackings, and burnings, John Brown and several of his sons rushed to the scene. Within a short time, Brown was one of the best-known of the "free state" guerrilla leaders. Grim, unsmiling, he preached a no-quarter doctrine of "an eye for an eye." After proslavery forces seized the initiative with a series of slayings and the burning and sacking of Lawrence, the antislavery center, Brown organized a retaliatory raid. At midnight, on May 26, 1856, men under Brown's command seized five proslavery men and slew them. Although Brown did not personally kill any of the men, the Pottawatomie killings, as they were called, are generally regarded as a blot on his record.

In Kansas, however, and later in Virginia, Brown acted on the theory that slavery was war. What he saw in Kansas and what he experienced there convinced him that drastic action was necessary to prevent the total triumph of the slave power. "Once," he said, "I saw three mutilated bodies [in Kansas]; two were dead and one still lived, but was riddled with twenty bullet holes and buck-shot holes; the two murdered men had been lying eighteen hours on the ground, a prey to the flies. One of these young men was my own son."

Then and later, Brown denied that he was motivated by ideas of personal vengeance, and the weight of evidence supports this. Almost all responsible historians agree on one fact: John Brown was prepared to give not only one son, but himself and, if necessary, his whole family to the cause which dominated his life.

After Kansas, Brown was convinced that it was necessary to "take the war into Africa." Resolving to seek the offensive, he sought financial support in the East. In Boston and New York, he conferred with Thomas Wentworth Higginson, Theodore Parker, Gerrit Smith, and other highly placed abolitionists. Satisfied, he returned to Kansas and recruited a cadre of nine white men and one black man. To this group, he outlined his plans for an attack on the Harpers Ferry area. He also told them that "God had created him to be the deliverer of slaves the same as Moses had delivered the children of Israel."

Establishing his cadre in a Quaker sanctuary in Springdale, Iowa, Brown returned to the East in January, 1858, to recruit men and money for the crowning event of his life. He turned first to black leaders, staying several weeks in the home of Frederick Douglass in Rochester, moving on later to the home of Mr. and Mrs. J. N. Gloucester in Brooklyn and the home of Stephen Smith in Philadelphia. Then, after a conference with his white backers, he hurried to Canada to scout the burgeoning black settlements. In St. Catherines, he met Harriet Tubman, who gave him information on secret routes and hiding places in the Maryland-Virginia-Delaware area. Convinced that there was "abundant material" (black recruits) in Canada for his purpose, he called a general convention in Chatham, Canada. The convention opened on May 8, 1858, with eleven white men and thirty-five black men in attendance. With Rev. William C. Munroe, black pastor of a Detroit church, in the chair, the convention speedily approved a plan for a revolutionary attack on the slave system of Virginia. A constitution, drafted by John Brown, was approved for government of the liberated area, and John Brown was elected commander-in-chief.

John Brown planned apparently to move from the convention to the assault on Harpers Ferry. But at that moment a defector leaked details of the plan to several politicians and community leaders. Brown's white backers, terrified, insisted that the raid be postponed. Reluctantly, Brown gave in and dispersed his men. Several of his men drifted to Ohio and other midwestern areas, but one, John E. Cook, went to Harpers Ferry to scout the terrain. Cook got a job as a locktender on the canal, married a local girl, and settled down to await the arrival of John Brown.

Brown was not idle. Returning to Kansas, he participated in several guerrilla campaigns. In December, 1858, he staged a Harpers Ferry rehearsal, invading Missouri and freeing eleven slaves. With a price on his head and a posse in hot pursuit, he led the slaves across Missouri, Iowa, Illinois, and Michigan, depositing them finally in Canada after an eleven-hundred-mile trip.

Refreshed by this interlude, Brown turned his face toward Harpers Ferry. In July, 1859, Brown, accompanied by two of his sons, appeared in the Harpers Ferry area. He said his name was Isaac Smith and that he was looking for a place to settle down. A townsman suggested the Kennedy Farm, which was about six miles from Harpers Ferry in Maryland. Finding the farm appropriate for his purposes, John Brown rented it and sent out calls for his men. It proved inordinately difficult, however, to revive interest in the project. The postponement had dampened the enthusiasm of some white rebels and had led some black rebels to question Brown's determination and resoluteness.

Brown planned apparently to make a blitzkrieg attack on Harpers Ferry and to retreat to the mountains, freeing slaves and establishing guerrilla footholds as he went. In order for the second phase of his plan to work, Brown needed, or believed he needed, a national black leader. It was extremely unlikely, as Brown knew, that slaves would flock to the banner of an unknown white man.

With that difficulty in mind, Brown sent an SOS call to Frederick Douglass, the major black leader of the day. The two men, along with Shields Green, a fugitive slave, and John H. Kagi, Brown's aide, met on Saturday and Sunday, August 16 and 17, in a deserted quarry near Chambersburg, Pennsylvania. Douglass was aware of the bare outlines of the plan, but he did not know that Brown intended to attack a U.S. arsenal. When this became clear, he indicated in no uncertain terms that he could not and would not endorse or participate in the raid. The two men argued for hours. Brown begged Douglass to accompany him, saying: "Come with me, Douglass. I will protect you with my life. When the bees begin to swarm, I'll need you to hive them." But Douglass was impervious to such pleas, for he considered Brown's new plan not only dangerous but provocative. After long hours of haggling, the two men parted, never to meet again. As Douglass was leaving, he asked Shields Green, his friend and traveling companion, if he were ready to go. Green, a tough, wiry man who had escaped from slavery in South Carolina, stood silent for a moment weighing the men and their motives. He looked from the cool, practical, and determined Douglass to the fiery, impractical, and determined Brown, from the young black leader to the old white leader. Then he said, quietly: "I believe I go wid de old man." Later, when John Brown was surrounded, Green had a chance to escape. A white man, a friend of John Brown, suggested flight, but Shields Green said: "I believe I go down wid de old man." And go he did, into the fray, onto the gallows, and into the grave.

Saddened by his inability to convince Douglass, but heartened by the blind faith of Shields Green and four other black men, John Brown returned to the Kennedy Farm to make preparations for the raid. By late September, most of his ill-starred crew were secreted in the attic of the farm. The group included two of John Brown's sons, Oliver and Owen, Shields Green and four other black men: John Anthony Copeland Jr., twenty-four, a free black man from Oberlin, Ohio; Osborn Perry Anderson, twenty-nine, a printer who had joined Brown in Canada; Lewis Sheridan Leary, twenty-four, a free man from Oberlin; and Dangerfield Newby, forty-four, of Fauquier County, Virginia. Newby, a former slave, had a wife and baby in slavery about thirty miles from Harpers Ferry. As late as August 16th, his wife had begged him to buy her and the baby as soon as possible "for if you do not get me somebody else will. Oh, Dear Dangerfield [she concluded], come this fall without fail, money or no money I want to see you so much; that is the one bright hope I have before me."

All of John Brown's men, black and white, were creatures of hope and indignation. Poets, dreamers, rebels, romantics: all—black and white—were willing to risk everything on one desperate roll of the dice. And all made their way to Kennedy Farm because of their faith in one white-haired old man. Osborne Anderson said as much in his book, *A Voice From Harpers Ferry*. "There was no milk and water sentimentality," he said, "no offensive contempt for the Negro, while working in his cause; the pulsations of each and every heart beat in harmony for the suffering and pleading slave. I thank God that I have been permitted to realize to its furthest, fullest extent, the moral, mental, physical, social harmony of an antislavery family, carrying out to the letter the principle of its antitype, the antislavery cause. . . ."

As D-Day drew near, pressures began to build up in John Brown's house. Neighbors were growing increasingly suspicious of activities at the house. It was noticed that "Isaac Smith," as John Brown called himself, did little real work. Even more suspicious were the large and mysterious crates which arrived at the farm at periodic intervals.

Almost all of the neighbors made furtive attempts to pry open the secret of Kennedy Farm. But "Isaac Smith" repelled intimacy, never entering anyone else's house and never inviting anyone into his. One neighbor, however, was insistent, calling at all hours of the day and night and barging into the house without knocking. One day she walked into the house and caught several of the men, including Shields Green, downstairs. Although she said nothing, John Brown realized that the fuse was growing short. Abruptly, he announced that the raid would begin on October 16, eight days ahead of schedule. The change in plans made it impossible for several men, black and white, to reach the scene; but time was of the essence now and John Brown did not intend to be cheated of his prize.

On Sunday, October 16, Brown rose earlier than usual and

called his men to worship. "He read a chapter from the Bible," Anderson reported, "applicable to the condition of the slave, and our duty as their brethren, and then offered up a fervent prayer to God to assist in the liberation of the bondsmen in that slaveholding land." After service, a council of war was held with O. P. Anderson, the black rebel, presiding. That afternoon final orders were given and that night, just before departing, John Brown said: "And now, gentlemen, let me impress this one thing upon your minds. You all know how dear life is to you, and how dear life is to your friends. And in remembering that consider that the lives of others are as dear to them as yours are to you. Do not, therefore, take the life of anyone if you can possibly avoid it; but if it is necessary to take life in order to save your own, then make sure work of it."

With that final admonition, the men gathered their weapons and started down the road to Harpers Ferry, a thumb of land on the left bank of the Potomac at the confluence of the Shenandoah and Potomac Rivers. The invading "army" approached the ferry from the Maryland side, Brown leading in a one horse wagon, followed by eighteen men marching two by two, guns at the ready. The rest of the party, three men, were left at the farm as a rearguard.

As the conspirators approached the bridge leading from Maryland into the ferry, squads fanned out to cut the telegraph wires and to capture the watchmen. Surprise, the central feature of the plan, served Brown well. Without firing a shot, Brown and his men entered the town and took command of the arsenal and armory. A crew was then sent a half-mile up the Shenandoah to take possession of the rifle works. Another crew was sent up-country to capture Colonel Lewis W. Washington, a great-grandnephew of George Washington, and to spread the word among the slaves. Always alert to the drama of his cause, Brown ordered his men to relieve Colonel Washington of a pistol presented to General Washington by Lafayette and a sword which, according to legend, was the gift of Frederick the Great to the "Father of his country." By Brown's specific orders, Colonel Washington was compelled to hand over the sword to the black rebel, Anderson. Then Washington and several of his slaves, who were told to come and fight for their freedom, set out for Harpers Ferry.

Historians have claimed that few slaves in the sparsely settled area joined the rebellion. But Anderson tells a different story. "On the road," he said, "we met some colored men, to whom we made known our purpose, when they immediately agreed to join us. They said they had long been waiting for an opportunity of the kind. [A member of the party] then asked them to go around among the colored people and circulate the news, when each started off in a different direction. The result was that many colored men gathered to the scene of action."

Meanwhile, the tempo of events picked up at the ferry. Several townsmen were captured and lodged in the armory; and a free black man, a porter at the train station, was mortally wounded after he failed to heed a command to "halt." It was a bad omen that the first man killed by the liberators was black.

By 1 A.M. on October 17th, John Brown and his men were in complete command of Harpers Ferry and the surrounding area. But speed was essential to the success of the plan and John Brown, for reasons he could never afterwards explain, decided to dawdle. Worse, he made several strategic decisions that doomed the raid. With incredible insouciance, he permitted a train to proceed through town. As a result, word of the raid reached Washington, D.C. and the capital of Virginia almost immediately. After committing this error, Brown, in violation of his own plan, retired to the armory and busied himself with the complaints and fears of his prisoners. Brown's aides frantically urged him to get on with the raid. But the old man seemed chained to the spot. He would say later that God had intervened and that "God's plan was beyond a doubt much better, otherwise

I should have held to my own."

In the hour of battle, this was small comfort to John Brown's men who watched, helplessly, as the Virginia militia shut off all avenues of retreat. With the arrival of U.S. Marines, under the command of Colonel Robert E. Lee, the trap was closed. Penned in the engine house, with his hostages and a handful of survivors, Brown made a last stand. But the Marines smashed into the engine house on the morning of October 18th and captured John Brown and six survivors. Five members of the party managed to escape and ten, including two of John Brown's sons, were killed.

The battle, however, was far from over and John Brown knew it. Had he died in the battle, had his mouth been stopped and his pen stilled, he probably would have gone down in history as a demented desperado. But by some miracle he survived his wounds, and he proved to be far more dangerous as an unarmed prisoner than he had ever been as an armed rebel. At the very beginning, John Brown the prisoner took charge of his captors. Even his foes marveled at the coolness and lucid fire of the man. Looking at him, lying bound and wounded on the prison floor, Governor John A. Wise of Virginia said: "He is the gamest man I ever met," adding: "And they are themselves mistaken who take him to be a madman. He is a bundle of the best nerves I ever saw cut and thrust and bleeding and in bonds. He is a man of clear head, of courage, fortitude, and simple ingenuousness. He is cool, collected, indomitable...."

Wise and his aides rushed John Brown and his men to trial on charges of treason, murder, and conspiring with slaves to rebel. Though wounded, John Brown was carried into court on a pallet to face his accusers. On November 2, he was convicted and sentenced to death. Calmly, deliberately, Brown rose from his bed of fate and delivered one of the most memorable speeches in courtroom history.

I have, may it please the Court, a few words to say.
In the first place, I deny everything but what I have all along admitted, —

the design on my part to free the slaves. . . . I have another objection; and that is, it is unjust that I should suffer such a penalty. Had I interfered in the manner which I admit, and which I admit has been fairly proved . . . had I so interfered in behalf of the rich, the powerful, the intelligent, the so-called great, or in behalf of any of their friends, — either father, mother, brother, sister, wife, or children, or any of that class, — and suffered and sacrificed what I have in this interference, it would have been all right; and every man in this court would have deemed it an act worthy of reward rather than punishment.

This court acknowledges, as I suppose, the validity of the law of God. I see a book kissed here which I suppose to be the Bible, or at least the New Testament. That teaches me that all things whatsoever I would that men should do to me, I should do even so to them. It teaches me, further, to "remember them that are in bonds, as bound with them." I endeavored to act up to that instruction. I say, I am yet too young to understand that God is any respector of persons. I believe that to have interfered as I have done — as I have always freely admitted I have done — in behalf of His despised poor, was not wrong, but right. Now, if it is deemed necessary that I should forfeit my life for the furtherance of the ends of justice, and mingle my blood further with the blood of my children and with the blood of millions in this slave country whose rights are disregarded by wicked, cruel, and unjust enactments, — I submit; so let it be done.

John Brown now had thirty days to live, and he used every one of them to good purpose. From his cell, he sent to his friends and to his family a series of dazzlingly brilliant letters which stirred the hearts of millions of Americans. Even his jailer wept as he read the last testament of the man who wrote: "I am, besides, quite cheerful, having (as I trust) 'the peace of God, which passeth all understanding' to 'rule my heart,' and the testimony (in some degree) of a good conscience that I have not lived altogether in vain. I can trust God with both the time and the manner of my death, believing as I now do that for me at this time to seal my testimony for God and humanity with my blood will do vastly more toward advancing the cause I have earnestly endeavored to promote, than all I have done in my life before."

Time and time again, John Brown returned to the idea of

sacrifice. To a friend, he wrote; "*Men* cannot *imprison*, or *chain;* or *hang* the soul. I go joyfully in behalf of millions that 'have no rights'...." He admitted that he had violated the laws of men but said that "whether it be right to obey God or men, judge ye."

As the hour of his death approached, Brown was overwhelmed by a sense of peace and contentment. "With me," he said, "all is joy." Indeed, he added, "I do not think that I have ever enjoyed life better than since my confinement here."

In a final letter, John Brown bade members of his family to "be of good cheer" "for He doeth all things well." Then, standing on the edge of eternity, he said: "Oh be determined at once to give your whole hearts to God ... & love ye the stranger *still.* It is ground of the utmost comfort to my mind to know that so many of you as have had the *opportunity*, have given full proof of your fidelity to the great family of men. Be *faithful* unto *death.* ...."

Until death, John Brown was faithful. He went on a clear, warm Friday — December 2, 1859 — to a gallows around which some fifteen hundred troops had been massed. John Brown regarded them for a moment, curiously. Then he lifted his eyes to the Blue Ridge Mountains and words burst from his lips. "This *is* a beautiful country," he said. "I never had the pleasure of seeing it before." The sheriff asked him if he wanted a private signal before the fatal moment. John Brown replied that it did not matter, really, "if only they would not keep him waiting too long." But they kept him waiting, twelve long painful minutes while the troops maneuvered into the exact formation. And all that time John Brown stood tall and erect as a mountain pine, showing his enemies how a brave man dies. At long last, the word came. A sharp blow from the sheriff's hatchet and John Brown swung between heaven and hell. Far away, in Massachusetts, Ralph Waldo Emerson saw the scene in his mind's eye and said that John Brown was a "new saint" whose martyrdom "will make the gallows as glorious as the cross."

God's Angry Man

John Brown's death and the execution of his aides, two black men and four whites, inflamed both the North and the South. Temperatures shot up in the North, and an air of panic and anxiety gripped the South. Neither in life nor in death could the South shake the spirit of the terrible-eyed old man. Before going to his death, he had penned a final message to the world.

I John Brown am now quite certain that the crimes of this *guilty land: will* never be purged *away;* but with Blood. I had *as I now think vainly* flattered myself that without *very much* bloodshed it might be done.

The old man proved to be a disastrously accurate prophet. Within two years, Union troops were marching through the heart of the South, singing:

John Brown's body lies a-mouldering in the grave
But his soul goes marching on.

WHITE ARCHITECTS

of

BLACK LIBERATION

———◆———

Charles Sumner
and
Thaddeus Stevens

> ...*anything for human rights is constitutional.*
>
> **CHARLES SUMNER**

THADDEUS STEVENS   *CHARLES SUMNER*

CHARLES SUMNER and Thaddeus Stevens were the best friends black Americans have had in public power.

More than any past or present politician, more even than the celebrated Lincoln, Sumner and Stevens were consumed by the cause of black liberation. As the dominant figures in Civil War and post-Civil War Congresses, Sumner and Stevens were primarily responsible for the legal scaffolding that undergirds equal rights in America.

In the turbulent Reconstruction era, Stevens was the virtual dictator of the House of Representatives and Sumner was, in Emerson's words, "the conscience of the Senate." Together and separately, alone and with like-minded colleagues, they made the U. S. Congress and the American people take the longest stride of soul in the history of the Commonwealth.

The Thirteenth, Fourteenth, and Fifteenth amendments are permanent testimonials to the courage and devotion of Sumner and Stevens; and the most daring proposals of contemporary legislators are only pale reflections of the civil rights bills they offered in the 1860's and 1870's. It was Stevens who captured the imagination of freedmen with a proposal for allocating "forty acres and a mule" to each freedman. It was Sumner who proposed a civil rights bill that would have banned segregation in schools, churches, cemeteries, public conveyances, and places of public accommodation. It was Sumner and Stevens who insisted that there could be no just and lasting racial peace except on the basis of equal rights for all men.

Both Sumner and Stevens were white, but both repudiated in principle and in practice the claims of white supremacy. Both were politicians, but both rose above the petty machinations of the typical politician. Both were lawyers, but both believed that laws were made for men and not men for laws. "...anything for human rights," Charles Sumner said, "is constitutional ... There can be no states rights against human rights."

Because they believed black men were human beings, because they acted on that belief in their public and private lives, Sumner and Stevens have been systematically vilified by a whole generation of historians. They have been denounced as "fanatics" who forced black suffrage and equal rights on the South, thereby precipitating "the horrors" of Reconstruction. The truth of the matter is that the failure of Reconstruction and America's current racial crisis are direct results of the failure to adopt and carry through the comprehensive Reconstruction plan articulated by Sumner and Stevens. This program included not only black suffrage and equal rights but also land reform and a complete revamping of the social system of the South.

It was no accident that Sumner and Stevens became the most articulate political advocates of the black cause. Both men were reared on the verities of the Declaration of Independence; and both men were, in a sense, products of the crisis they transcended. Stevens, the older of the two, was born on April 4, 1792, in Danville, Vermont, to Jacob Stevens, a poor surveyor, and his wife, Sarah. He was born with a clubfoot and this deformity colored his whole life. Shy, sensitive, embarrassed by his deformity, Stevens developed a passion for the poor, the disinherited, and the driven-against-the-wall. He was not a happy boy. A friend who knew him in those days remembered him as "still and quiet-like, different from the rest of the boys," who would "laugh at him, boy-like, and mimic his limping walk." As a defense mechanism, Stevens secreted a hard shell of cynicism which encased and protected his inner core of compassion and sensitivity. Ever afterwards, his sharp tongue and his brusque forbidding exterior would hold the world at arm's length.

Like many other sensitive and disturbed youths, Stevens hid his hurt in books. He was a good, if not spectacular, student at the grade schools of Peacham, Vermont, and at Dartmouth College, where he was graduated in 1814. Moving on to Pennsylvania after graduation, he taught school for a year and then opened a law office in Gettysburg. Aloof, withdrawn, his energy focused almost entirely on the problem of making a living, Stevens soon moved to the forefront of the professional community in Gettysburg. Within nine years after settling in Gettysburg, he was the largest real estate owner in the county. Stevens later became the principal owner of an iron business and moved his base of operations to the larger city of Lancaster.

With his base secure, the young lawyer entered politics and won election to the Pennsylvania General Assembly. Opposed to all special privileges, he distinguished himself in a bitter fight against secret societies. Standing alone in one session, he repulsed foes of public education and won the title of father of the common school system in Pennsylvania.

As a legislator and private citizen, Stevens was an early champion of the free black man and the fugitive slave. He waged an unsuccessful fight for universal suffrage, and he assisted individual black men financially and spiritually. Despite his heavy schedule, Stevens always had time to take the cases of fugitive slaves. When courts ruled against him, Stevens usually purchased the freedom of his clients.

During this same period, Charles Sumner was moving toward his encounter with reality. Sumner was born into comfortable circumstances in Boston, on January 6, 1811. Like Stevens, Sumner was a bookworm; unlike Stevens, however, he used books as a crutch. It would be said later, with some justification, that his speeches were overloaded with quotations and classical allusions.

Something of a dandy, Sumner made his mark in Boston social circles and went on to Harvard University and the Harvard University Law School. He then made an extended tour of European cities before settling down to law practice in Boston. Finding the traditional fare of the lawyer somewhat restrictive, Sumner was soon engaged in unpopular causes as an advocate and agitator. He distinguished himself in the late 1840's in one of the first separate-but-equal school suits, arguing unsuccessfully for a group of black Boston parents.

Sumner, like Stevens, would have been an extraordinary man in any era. But it seems likely that he and Stevens would have been lost to posterity had it not been for the issue of slavery, which began to exert a persuasive influence on the lives of men in the 1830's and 1840's. In these years, the South inaugurated an ominous policy of external expansion. The net result was that a variety of issues — the Mexican War, the annexation of Texas, the fugitive slave bill — stretched the fabric of the Union to the breaking point and forced a realignment of parties. It was in this climate that both Sumner and Stevens found the consuming passion of their lives.

Stevens, who was already a political power in Pennsylvania, came to the fore first, winning election in 1849 to the national House of Representatives. In his maiden speech, he announced a new policy of open Northern resistance to the steady advance of the slave power. "How often," he wondered, "had these walls been profaned and the North insulted by insolent threats that if Congress legislated against the Southern will it would be disregarded, resisted to extremity and the Union destroyed? During the present session, we have been more than once told amid raving excitement that if we dared to legislate in a certain way the South would teach the North a lesson." With cool

defiance, Stevens told the South: "You have too often in-
timidated Congress. You have more than once frightened the
tame North for its propriety and found dough-faces enough to
be your tools." That day, Stevens said, had passed. Hereafter,
he concluded, the South would have to contend with men.

With this speech, Stevens became the acknowledged leader
of antislavery forces in the House. For the rest of the term, he
fought a brilliant campaign against compromise and timidity
in Northern ranks. But the tide of Northern appeasement was
too strong for Stevens to hold back. After passage of the
Compromise of 1850, which was designed, in part, to shut off
debate on the question of slavery, Stevens retired from the
House and returned to Lancaster.

Far from shutting off debate, the Compromise of 1850
widened the controversy, particularly in Massachusetts, where
Charles Sumner waded out into the depths as a leader of men.
Sumner, who had won some fame as an orator, announced that
he would not obey the Fugitive Slave law, which was an integral
part of the Compromise of 1850. "We are told," he said, "that
the slavery question is settled....Nothing, sir, can be settled
which is not right. *Nothing can be settled which is against freedom.*"
Sumner went on to say that "the friends of freedom cannot
lightly bestow their confidence." He added: "They can put
trust only in men of tried character and inflexible will. Three
things at least they must require; the first is *backbone*; the second
is *backbone*; and the third is *backbone*. When I see a person of
upright character and pure soul yielding to a temporizing policy,
I cannot but say, *He wants backbone.* When I see a person talking
loudly against slavery in private, but hesitating in public and
failing in the time of trial, I say, *He wants backbone.* When I see
a person leaning upon the action of a political party and never
venturing to think for himself, I say, *He wants backbone.* Wanting
this they all want the courage, constancy, firmness, which are
essential to the support of principle. Let no such man be
trusted."

Whatever Sumner lacked, he did not lack backbone. Taking a leading position in the gathering controversy, he was elected in 1851 to the Senate, which he made a forum for the anti-slavery cause. In a series of great speeches, he said that slavery presented a clear and present danger to the free institutions of the North. Like Stevens, who returned to the House in 1858 as a member of the new Republican party, Sumner said that the Declaration of Independence argued against any artificial distinctions between man and man. Angered by Sumner's speeches, the South struck back. On Thursday, May 22, 1856, while Sumner was writing letters at his desk on the Senate floor, a proslavery congressman, Preston Brooks of South Carolina, attacked him with a heavy cane. Brooks rained blows on Sumner's head until he collapsed on the Senate floor. This incident, following hard on the heels of the bitter North-South struggle for Kansas, inflamed the political climate of the North. Sumner, who was seriously injured in the attack, remained away from the Senate for more than three years, and Massachusetts left his seat vacant as a reproach to the South.

During Sumner's absence, Stevens and other antislavery congressmen continued the fight for black liberation. There was, at the same time, a widening of the circle of combatants, as evidenced by the steady growth of the Republican party. When, in 1859, Sumner returned to the Senate, the stage was set for the North-South rupture which occurred after the election of Abraham Lincoln.

Both Sumner and Stevens saw the Civil War as an opportunity to complete the Revolution of 1776. From the beginning of the conflict to their death, Sumner and Stevens waged an unceasing battle for the ending of slavery and the granting of equal rights to all men. Far in advance of Lincoln and the country, Sumner and Stevens educated Lincoln and the country to a policy of black emancipation. To them, as much as to the more conservative Lincoln, black people owe their freedom.

Charles Sumner and Thaddeus Stevens

After issuance of the Emancipation Proclamation, the two legislators turned to the problems of Reconstruction. By this time, the center of initiative had passed to Congress, and Sumner and Stevens were among the most powerful men in the land. As chairman of the powerful Ways and Means Committee of the House, Stevens was in undisputed control of that body. He used his great powers to wrench control of Reconstruction from the executive and to focus the country's mind on the "radical" reconstruction of the South. Blunt and sarcastic in debate and brilliant in behind-the-scenes maneuvering, he won his way by sheer force of will. His favorite stratagem was to move suspension of the rules so the House could go into a Committee of the Whole to consider his bills. Before the vote, he would move that general debate on the bill be closed in an hour or thirty minutes. On one occasion, he even limited debate on a major bill to thirty seconds.

Stevens was a political being, dedicated to the art of the possible. Sumner, on the other hand, was a moralist to whom nothing was impossible. "I am in morals," he was given to saying, "not politics." Unlike Stevens, who loved the give and take of politics, Sumner took the high road, lecturing his colleagues on history and morals. By constantly raising an issue and forcing his colleagues to go on record, he usually won his way. So insistent was Sumner that one of his colleagues asked him to give the Senate "one day without the nigger."

As long as Sumner lived, the Senate resounded with the cry of the black man. By amending an act, he stopped discrimination on streetcars in Washington D.C. The next year he stopped exclusion of witnesses on account of color in the federal courts. He also introduced and carried a bill to amend the law which provided that "no one other than a free white person should be employed to carry the mail." The Massachusetts senator also played a pivotal role in abolishing slavery in Washington D.C. and carried the recognition of Haiti and Liberia as independent states. In gratitude, Haiti voted him a medal and hung his portrait in its state house.

Sumner, like Stevens, was at the height of his power in the dying days of the Civil War. An English traveler described him in the following terms. "That great, sturdy, English-looking figure, with the broad, massive forehead, over which the rich mass of nutbrown hair, streaked here and there with a line of gray, hangs loosely; with the deep, blue eyes and the strangely winning smile, half bright, half full of sadness. He is a man whom you would notice amongst other men, and whom, not knowing, you would turn round and look at as he passed by you. . . . A child would ask him the time in the streets, and a woman would come to him unbidden for protection." Though Sumner was favored by nature, he was essentially a lonely man who married late in life and was soon divorced.

Stevens never married. His homes in Lancaster and in Washington were presided over by a black housekeeper, Lydia Hamilton Smith, an attractive widow. Because Stevens called his housekeeper "Mrs. Smith," gossips said there was more to their relationship than met the eye. Indifferent to and contemptuous of public opinion, Stevens disdainfully ignored the gossips and went his lonely way.

Cynical and tough-talking, Stevens was a man with few close friends. His chief form of relaxation was gambling. The story is told of the time he emerged from a gambling house after a profitable night and met a preacher who asked for a donation for his church. Without a word, Stevens handed the preacher a fistful of bills. As the preacher walked away, Stevens remarked to a friend: "The Lord moves in mysterious ways, His wonders to perform."

No respecter of idols and myths, tart-tongued, indifferent to both status and color, Stevens was the chief architect of the constitutional revolution which yielded the Fourteenth and Fifteenth amendments. Acting with the boldness that characterized his entire life, he wrested control of Reconstruction from President Andrew Johnson and vested it in the Joint Congressional Committee. From this committee, with Stevens leading the way, came the momentous Fourteenth and Fifteenth amendments. Stevens also waged a long and unsuccessful fight for forty acres of land for each freedman. "The whole fabric of Southern society must be changed," he said, "and it never can be done if this opportunity is lost.... How can republican institutions, free schools, free churches, free social intercourse, exist in a mingled community of nabobs and serfs, of the owners of twenty thousand acre manors with lordly palaces and the occupants of narrow huts inhabited by 'low white trash'? If the South is ever to be made a safe republic let her lands be culti- vated by the toil of the owners or the free labor of intelligent citizens. This must be done even though it drives her nobility into exile! If they go, all the better. It will be hard to persuade the owner of ten thousand acres of land, who drives a coach and four, that he is not degraded by sitting at the same table or in the same pew, with the embrowned and hard-handed farmer who has himself cultivated his own thriving homestead of 150 acres. The country would be well rid of the proud, bloated and defiant rebels.... The foundations of their institutions ... must be broken up and relaid, or all of our blood and treasure have been spent in vain."

Stevens' Reconstruction plan was part of a comprehensive program for the reordering of the relations between black and white Americans. He told the House: "We have turned, or are about to turn, loose four million slaves without a hut to shelter them or a cent in their pockets. The infernal laws of slavery have prevented them from acquiring an education, under- standing the commonest laws of contract, or of managing the ordinary business life. This Congress is bound to provide for them until they can take care of themselves. If we do not furnish them with homesteads, and hedge them around with protective laws; if we leave them to the legislation of their late masters, we had better have left them in bondage."

Stevens went on to denounce the idea that this is a white man's country. "Governor Perry of South Carolina and other provisional governors and orators proclaim that 'this is the white man's government'.... Demagogues of all parties, even some high in authority, gravely shout, 'this is the white man's government.' What is implied by this? That one race of men are to have the exclusive rights forever to rule this nation, and to exercise all acts of sovereignty, while all other races and nations and colors are to be their subjects, and have no voice in making the laws and choosing the rulers by whom they are to be governed.... Our fathers repudiated the whole doctrine of the legal superiority of families or races, and proclaimed the equality of men before the law. Upon that they created a revolution and built the Republic.... It is our duty to complete their work. If this Republic is not now made to stand on their great principles, it has no honest foundation, and the Father of all men will still shake it to its center. If we have not been sufficiently scourged for our national sin to teach us to do justice to all God's creatures, without distinction of race or color, we must expect the still more heavy vengeance of an offended Father...."

Stevens' vision of a complete reconstruction of the South was too bold for most men, and the equalitarian legislator, who was known as "The Great Commoner," admitted defeat in a great House speech. "In my youth," he said, "in my manhood, in my old age, I had fondly dreamed that when any fortunate chance should have broken for a while the foundation of our institutions, and released us from obligations the most tyrannical that ever man imposed in the name of freedom, that the intelligent, pure and just men of the Republic, true to their professions and their consciences, would have so remodeled all our institutions as to have freed them from every vestige of human oppression, of inequality of rights, of the recognized degradation of the poor, and the superior caste of the rich. In short, that no distinction would be tolerated in this purified republic but what arose from merit and conduct. This bright dream has vanished 'like the baseless fabric of a vision.' I find that we shall be obliged to be content with patching up the worst portions of the ancient edifice, and leaving it, in many of its parts, to be swept through by the tempests, frosts and the storms of despotism."

In the patching up, Stevens was aided enormously by Sumner who, single-handed, defeated every compromise that evaded the issue of black suffrage. Said he: "Equality of rights is the standing promise of nature to man. . . . In harmony with the promise of Nature is the promise of our fathers recorded in the Declaration of Independence. It is the twofold promise; first, that all are equal in rights; and, secondly, that just government stands only on the consent of the governed,—being the two great political commandments on which hang all laws and constitutions. Keep these truly and you will keep all. Write them in your statutes; write them in your hearts. This is the great and only final settlement of all existing questions."

Sumner and Stevens went to their graves fighting for a final and just solution of the racial problem. Shortly before his death, Sumner inaugurated a fight for a civil rights bill which would have barred segregation in public accommodations. On his death bed, surrounded by Frederick Douglass and other black friends, he whispered his last words: "Take care of my civil rights bill—take care of it—you must do it." Sumner died on March 11, 1874. His civil rights bill was enacted by Congress in March, 1875.

Thaddeus Stevens had said that he intended to "die hurrahing." And he did. After his death on August 11, 1868, he was buried in a black cemetery. The stone above the ground bears words that invoke the meaning of the great fight that he and his colleague, Charles Sumner, waged:

White Architects of Black Liberation

I repose in this quiet and secluded spot,
not from any natural preference for solitude,
but finding other cemeteries
limited by charter rules as to race.
I have chosen this that I might illustrate in my death
the principles which I advocated through a long life.
Equality of Man before his Creator.

FATHER
of the
PROTEST MOVEMENT

Frederick Douglass

If there is no struggle, there is no progress.

FREDERICK DOUGLASS

FREDERICK DOUGLASS

ON A HOT DAY in August, 1864, a prominent politician entered the White House and paused in the President's outer office. "It was dark," Judge Joseph T. Mills wrote later, "and there in a corner I saw a man quietly reading who possessed a remarkable physiognomy."

The man awed Judge Mills.

"I was riveted to the spot," he said, adding: "I stood and stared at him. He raised his flashing eyes and caught me in the act I was compelled to speak. Said I, 'Are you the President?' 'No,' replied the stranger, 'I am Frederick Douglass.'"

It was an honest mistake.

Frederick Douglass was in Washington to see Abraham Lincoln. He was not the President, but, under different circumstances, he could have been. He had all the gifts — presence, passion, bearing, brilliance — all the gifts save one: he was nonwhite. Color — an accident of birth — barred him from the highest prize, but it did not prevent him from becoming one of the noblest of all Americans.

Born in the lowest position of society, Douglass emancipated himself and became an orator, an abolitionist, an editor, a politician, a seer, and a prophet. Born black and hungry in a society that forbade slaves to read, he lifted himself by his own efforts and became one of the great names in an age that abounds in greatness. For fifty years, from 1845 to 1895, he was in the forefront of the fight for human freedom. During this period, he laid the foundation for the black protest movement.

Although he died in 1895, Frederick Douglass speaks with uncommon force to the problems of this age. One hundred and ten years ago, he was staging sit-ins on Massachusetts railroads. One hundred and six years ago, he was leading a fight for integrated schools in Rochester, New York. One hundred years ago, he was denouncing hypocrisy and fraud with pre-Baldwin fury:

"The whole history of the progress of human liberty shows that all concessions yet made to her august claims, have been born of earnest struggle. . . . If there is no struggle, there is no progress. Those who profess to favor freedom and yet deprecate agitation, are men who want crops without plowing up the ground, they want rain without thunder and lightning. They want the ocean without the awful roar of its many waters.

"This struggle may be a moral one, or it may be a physical one, or it may be both moral and physical, but it must be a struggle. Power concedes nothing without a demand. It never did and it never will. . . . Men may not get all they pay for in this world, but they must certainly pay for all they get. If we ever get free from the oppressions and wrongs heaped upon us, we must pay for their removal. We must do this by labor, by suffering, by sacrifice, and if needs be, by our lives and the lives of others."

More important than the eloquence of Douglass' words was the eloquence of his life. He was born Frederick Augustus Washington Bailey in February, 1817, on the eastern shore of Maryland. He never knew his father (who was rumored to be his master) and he only saw his mother five or six times. Slavery, he said once, abolished both fatherhood and motherhood. As a child, he knew the brutality and degradation of slavery. He knew hunger and pain, and he saw his aunt and other black men and women whipped.

A stroke of luck sent Douglass to Baltimore, Maryland, where he learned at an early age that knowledge is power. His mistress wanted to teach him the alphabet, but his master forbade it. "Give a nigger an inch," he said, "and he will take an ell.... Learning would spoil the best nigger in the world." The slave boy, not yet ten years old, brooded over this message and concluded that words were weapons. He hid dirty pages in his pockets and when no one was looking, he extracted the pages and spelled out the magic words. Three years later, Douglass came across a book called *The Columbian Orator*, which gave him an insight into his own condition. *The Columbian Orator* told Douglass who he was and how he got that way and what he could do about it. "With that book," he said, "I penetrated to the secret of all slavery and all oppression and perceived my own human nature and the facts of my past and present experiences."

Later, while still a slave, Douglass learned that power has its limitations. This was an extraordinary discovery and it changed the whole course of his life. It happened this way. He refused to buckle down to his master and was sent to a professional Negro-breaker, who specialized in destroying the spirit of slaves who would not submit to the slave regime. The Negro-breaker's name was Edward Covey, and Covey was *good* at his trade. He worked Douglass until he was ready to drop from exhaustion and whipped him until he bowed and smiled. But worms — and slaves and Negroes — turn. One day, Douglass tells us, he turned and made a desperate last stand. The two men grappled to an indecisive draw. Covey stalked off and never afterwards touched Douglass. Looking back on this incident many years later, Douglass said: "A man without force, is without the essential dignity of humanity. Human nature is so constituted, that it cannot honor a helpless man, although it can pity him; and even this it cannot do long if the signs of power do not arise. He only can understand the effect of this combat on my spirit who has himself incurred something, hazarded something, in repelling the unjust and cruel aggressions of a tyrant.... I had reached the point, at which I was not afraid to die. This spirit made me a free man in fact, while I remained a slave in form. When a slave cannot be flogged, he is more than half free." Douglass added: "Experience proves that those are oftenest abused who can be abused with the greatest impunity. Men are whipped oftenest who are whipped easiest."

Four years later, at the age of twenty-one, Douglass escaped from slavery. In 1838, he borrowed a sailor suit and an official-looking paper with a big American eagle on it. Grabbing a train, he traveled to New York, flashing his eagle-stamped paper as he went. In New York, he immediately married Anna Murray, a charming, free black woman from Baltimore who had followed him to New York. With the help of underground agents, the young couple settled in two rooms on "M" Street overlooking Buzzard's Bay in New Bedford, Massachusetts. One of Douglass' friends, Nathan Johnson, a literary fan of Sir Walter Scott, suggested that Douglass abandon his slave name and adopt the name of one of Scott's characters. Douglass agreed and Frederick Augustus Washington Bailey began his life as a free man under the name of Frederick Douglass.

For almost three years, Douglass lived and worked in New Bedford, where his first children were born. During this period, Douglass supported his family by sawing wood, waiting tables, working on the docks, and at a local brass foundry. He recalled later that he often nailed newspapers to the post near his bellows and studied while he was performing his work.

It did not take Douglass long to realize that he had escaped from the chattel slavery of the South into the caste slavery of the North. Outraged by the remembered wrongs of chattel slavery and the experienced wrongs of caste slavery, Douglass allied himself with the currents of the emerging abolitionist movement. He subscribed to Garrison's *Liberator* and attended meetings held by local Negroes. By 1841 Douglass was a leader of the black community of New Bedford. It was in August of that year that William Lloyd Garrison and other abolitionist leaders heard him speak at an abolitionist convention in Nantucket. Garrison was overwhelmed by Douglass' speech which he said "would have done honor to Patrick Henry." Garrison and his aides offered Douglass $450 a year to become a lecturer for the Massachusetts Anti-Slavery Society. Douglass accepted and at the age of twenty-four joined the phalanx of black and white men who were waging an intensive cold war against slavery. White abolitionists like William Lloyd Garrison and free black men like Charles Lennox Remond were in the forefront of the movement, but they did not have the first-hand knowledge that Douglass had; and their speeches lacked his concreteness and fire.

Douglass on the platform was a sight to see. He was a good-looking man, tall, well-built, with olive skin and a halo of hair worn long in the African style. His physical presence moved people. So did the rolling thunder of his voice. By turns humorous, dolorous, and indignant, he transported his audience to slave row. A master mimic, he could make people *laugh* at a slave owner preaching the duties of Christian obedience, could make them *see* the humiliation of a black maiden ravished by a brutal slaveowner, could make them *hear* the sobs of a mother separated from her child. Through him, people could *live* slavery. "White men and black men," William Wells Brown said, "had talked against slavery, but none had ever spoken like Frederick Douglass."

Life in this age was not easy for a white agitator: it was impossible for a black man. Douglass was roughed up by pro-slavery thugs; his right hand was broken; he was thrown down steps. But he took his knocks and stood his ground. It was difficult in this age to find a hall that would let a black abolitionist use its facilities. In Grafton, Massachusetts, he took a bell and made the rounds announcing his own meeting. In Dorchester, New York, Douglass took a stand under a tree and began addressing five people. By the time he warmed up, he had an audience of five hundred.

Within a few years, Douglass was a household name. In 1845, on publication of his first book, *The Autobiography of Frederick Douglass*, Douglass was forced to flee the country to avoid recapture by his owner. During this enforced exile, Douglass traveled to England, Ireland, and Scotland, was feted by ladies, lords, and earls. In a famous letter from Ireland, Douglass painted a harsh picture of America: "In thinking of America, I sometime find myself admiring her bright blue sky — her grand old woods — her fertile fields — her beautiful rivers — her mighty lakes, and star-crowned mountains. But my rapture is soon checked, my joy is soon turned to mourning. When I remember that all is cursed with the infernal spirit of slaveholding, robbery and wrong, — when I remember that with the waters of her noblest rivers, the tears of my brethren are borne to the ocean, disregarded and forgotten, and that her most fertile fields drink daily of the warm blood of my outraged sisters, I am filled with unutterable loathing, and led to reproach myself that any thing could fall from my lips in praise of such a land. America will not allow her children to love her. She seems bent on compelling those who would be her warmest friends, to be her worst enemies. May God give her repentance before it is too late, is the ardent prayer of my heart. I will continue to pray, labor and wait, believing that she cannot always be insensible to the dictates of justice, or deaf to the voice of humanity."

Douglass' reception was so warm in England, Ireland, and Scotland that he was tempted to remain abroad. But in an eloquent farewell speech at London Tavern, he said: "I choose rather to go home; to return to America. I glory in the conflict, that I may hereafter exalt in the victory. I know that victory is certain. I go, turning my back upon the ease, comfort, and respectability which I might maintain even here, ignorant as I am. Still, I will go back, for the sake of my brethren. I go to suffer with them; to toil with them; to endure insult with them; to lift up my voice in their behalf; to speak and write in their vindication; and struggle in their ranks for that emancipation which shall yet be achieved by the power of truth and of principle for that oppressed people."

So, turning his back on ease, comfort and respectability, Douglass returned to America. For almost six years, he had labored in the Garrison vineyard. Now he stepped out on his own. In 1847, he started publishing the *North Star* in Rochester, New York. From that year until the abolition of slavery, he was in the forefront of the abolitionist ranks.

Then and later, Douglass was a formidable advocate.

First of all and most important of all, Douglass was a man, in the deepest and truest sense of that much abused word. Douglass knew that to be a man is to be, precisely, responsible. He knew, too, that manhood is founded on self-respect and self-esteem. Frederick Douglass did not doubt himself, nor did he apologize for his place of birth or the color of his mother's skin

He was involved. He did not isolate himself from the masses. Wherever he went, the black man went with him. He bitterly criticized free Negroes—and there were many—who were indifferent to the antislavery cause. Free Negroes and slaves, he said, were chained together and would rise or fall together. His mission, he said, was "to stand up for the downtrodden, to speak for the dumb, and to remember those in bond as bound with me." He added: "It is more than a figure of speech to say, that [Negroes] are as a people chained together. We are one people—one in general complexion, one in common degradation, one in popular estimation. As one rises, all must rise; and as one falls, all must fall.... Every one of us should be ashamed to consider himself free, while his brother is a slave.—The wrongs of our brethren should be our constant theme. There should be no time too precious, no calling too holy, no place too sacred, to make room for the cause."

Douglass was consumed by the cause. Wherever he was, he sought out the struggle and involved himself in it. As superintendent of the Underground Railroad in Rochester, New York, he participated in the dangerous — and illegal — work of helping fugitive slaves escape into Canada.

He was militant. He not only told the truth, but he also lived it. He refused to accept segregation and discrimination; he assumed that every door open to a human being was open to him; and, if turned away, he made an issue of it. When asked to leave a Jim Crow car, he would refuse to move. The conductor usually called assistants who would drag Douglass out of the car along with several seats he always managed to hold onto.

He was independent. No man dictated to him, and no party or faction could silence his voice. Although he was ambitious, although he hungered and thirsted after political office, he never sold his principles. No dream of honors, no hope of office, could still his advocacy of freedom. "I am a Republican," he said once, "but I am not a Republican right or wrong."

And he was catholic. He was a universal man and he refused, he said, to allow himself "to be insensible to the wrongs and sufferings of any part of the great family of man." He fought for women's suffrage, free speech, "poor barefoot Ireland," and the Chinese; and he opposed flogging in the Navy, monopolies, and capital punishment. "I base no man's rights," he said, "upon his color, and plead no man's rights because of his color. My objection to slavery is not that it sinks a Negro to the condition of a brute, but that it sinks a man to that condition." Douglass realized, however, that individuality is universality. He realized that a man is most human when he is most himself. And he made no apologies for raising inconvenient questions. When he was rich in honors and money, he accepted an invitation to speak in Ohio; but he warned the sponsors that he did not intend to bite his tongue. Black people, he said, "still need the help of all who can say a word in their behalf. If I come to you in July, I shall bring the colored man with me."

Throughout this period, Douglass took the lead in militant, direct action against the chattel slavery of the South and the caste slavery of the North. In 1850, for example, he staged a school boycott in Rochester, New York. He explained later: "[My children] were not allowed in the public school in the district in which I lived, owned property, and paid taxes, but were compelled, if they went to a public school, to go over to the other side of the city to an inferior colored school. I hardly need say that I was not prepared to submit tamely to this proscription ... so I had them taught at home for a while.... Meanwhile I went to the people with the question, and created a considerable agitation. I sought and obtained a hearing before the Board of Education, and after repeated efforts with voice and pen, the doors of the public schools were opened and colored children were permitted to attend them in common with others."

In an age of danger and doubt, Douglass and other black abolitionists came to grips with dilemmas which lie deep in the Afro-American heart. Douglass asked the old and insistent question: "How can I sing the Lord's song in a strange land?" The answers revolved around the traditional trilogy: ballots, bullets, or Bibles, and Iago's injunction: "Go, make money." The followers of William Lloyd Garrison condemned "complexional institutions" (black churches, lodges, schools, newspapers and conventions). The Garrisonians also abandoned political action and advocated a campaign based on passive resistance and moral force.

After 1851, Douglass favored ballots, if possible, and bullets, if necessary. He was an opportunist on the issue of "complexional institutions." He demanded complete integration, but if circumstances made this impossible, he unhesitatingly recommended special institutions. At stake here was a bitter issue of power. Douglass was an independent man who felt uncomfortable in a subsidiary role; he demanded a share in the "generalship" of the movement. In a statement which anticipated the contemporary black power movement, he said: "If we are ever elevated, our elevation will have been accomplished through our own instrumentality. The history of other oppressed nations will confirm us in this assertion. No People that has solely depended upon foreign aid, or rather, upon the efforts of those in any way identified with the oppressor, to undo the heavy burdens, ever stood forth in the attitude of Freedom. Some one, imbued with the spirit of human freedom, from among themselves, has arisen to lead them on to victory. *They* have dashed their fetters to the ground."

When Garrison and other white abolitionists refused to share the "generalship" of the movement, Douglass struck out on his own. He believed that he and other black abolitionists could make a positive contribution by proving that black people were active rather than passive cogs in the anti-slavery machinery. He said that "... the man who has *suffered the wrong* is the man to demand redress — that the man STRUCK is the man to CRY OUT — and that he who has *endured the cruel pangs of Slavery* is the man to *advocate Liberty*. It is evident that we must be our own representatives and advocates, not exclusively, but peculiarly — not distinct from, but in connection with our white friends."

Douglass was scornful of the missionary mentality of some white abolitionists. "The relation," he said, "subsisting between the white and black people of this country is the vital question of the age.... Here, a man must be hot or be accounted cold, or, perchance, something worse than hot or cold. The lukewarm and the cowardly, will be rejected by earnest men on either side of the controversy. The cunning man who avoids it, to gain the favor of both parties, will be rewarded with scorn; and the timid man who shrinks from it, for fear of offending either party, will be despised. To the lawyer, the preacher, the politician, and to the man of letters, there is no neutral ground. He that is not for us, is against us."

Frederick Douglass

As a theorist and advocate, Douglass stressed the structural roots of racism. He said it was libelous to call the race problem the Negro problem. The real problem, he said, was the white problem. The real problem, he said, was the determination of white Americans to live out of the blood and the labor of black Americans. The only solution, he told black Americans, was struggle. He urged black Americans to pool their resources in a massive crusade against racism. Although he considered the ballot indispensable, he did not neglect economic power. Economic power and political power, he said, were linked, for political power could translate itself into economic power and vice versa. "Every blow of the sledgehammer, wielded by a sable arm, is a powerful blow in support of our cause," he said. "Every colored mechanic, is, by virtue of circumstances, an elevator of his race. Every house built by black men is a strong tower against the allied hosts of prejudice.... It is impossible for us to attach too much importance to this aspect of the subject.... Understand this, that independence is an essential condition of respectability. To be dependent, is to be degraded. Men may indeed pity us, but they cannot respect us."

In the midst of the terrible economic crisis of the 1850's, Douglass told black Americans that it was necessary to find new ways of making a living, adding: "The old avocations, by which colored men obtained a livelihood, are rapidly, unceasingly and inevitably passing into other hands; every hour sees the black man elbowed out of employment....

"White men are becoming house-servants, cooks, and stewards on vessels—at hotels. They are becoming porters, stevedores, wood-sawyers, hod-carriers, brick-makers, white-washers and barbers, so that blacks can scarcely find the means of subsistence —a few years ago, and a *white* barber would have been a curiosity—now their poles stand on every street. Formerly blacks were almost the exclusive coachmen in wealthy families: this is so no longer, white men are now employed, and for aught we see, they fill their servile station with an obsequiousness as profound as that of the blacks. The readiness and ease with which they adapt themselves to these conditions ought not to be lost sight of by the colored people. The meaning is very important, and we should learn it. We are taught our insecurity by it. Without the means of living, life is a curse, and leaves us at the mercy of the oppressor to become his debased slave. Now, colored men, what do you mean to do, for you must do something? ... *One thing is certain: we must find new methods of obtaining a livelihood, for the old ones are failing us very fast.*"

Despite the intensity of the crisis, Douglass was contemptuous of the back-to-Africa plan of Martin Delany, another pioneer black nationalist. As he said later, "It is all nonsense to talk about the removal of eight millions of the American people from their homes in America to Africa. The expense and hardships, to say nothing of the cruelty attending such a measure, would make success impossible. The American people are wicked, but they are not fools; they will hardly be disposed to incur the expenses, to say nothing of the injustice which the measure demands.... The bad thing about it is, that it has, of late, owing to persecution, begun to be advocated by colored men of acknowledged ability and learning, and every little while some white statesman becomes its advocate. These gentlemen will doubtless have their opinion of me; I certainly have mine of them. My opinion is, that if they are sensible, they are insincere; and if they are sincere, they are not sensible. They know, or they ought to know, that it would take more money than the cost of the late war, to transport even one half of the coloured people of the United States to Africa. Whether intentionally or not, they are, as I think, simply trifling with an afflicted people. They urge them to look for relief where they ought to know that relief is impossible."

Douglass believed that black and white were inseparably joined. "My friends, the destiny of the colored Americans ... is the destiny of America. We shall never leave you. The allot-

ments of Providence seem to make the black man of America
the open book out of which the American people are to learn
lessons of wisdom, power and goodness — more sublime and
glorious than any yet attained by the nations of the old or the
new world. Over the bleeding back of the American bondsman
we shall learn mercy. In the extreme difference of color and
features of the Negro and the Anglo-Saxon, shall be learned the
highest ideas of the sacredness of man, and the fullness and
perfection of human brotherhood."

And again:

"We are here, and here we are likely to be. To imagine that we
should ever be eradicated is absurd and ridiculous. We can be
modified, changed, assimilated, but never extinguished. We
repeat, therefore, that we are here; and that this is our country;
and the question for the philosophers and statesmen of the land
ought to be, What principle should dictate the policy of the
nation toward us? We shall neither die out, nor be driven out;
but shall go with this people, either as a testimony against them,
or as an evidence in their favor throughout their generation. . . ."

America's failure to make a meaningful response to the
abolitionist campaign infuriated Douglass and he lashed out
with the fire and the eloquence of the Old Testament prophets.
Speaking at Rochester, New York, on July 5, 1852, he indicted
every structure of power in America. "What," he asked, "to the
American slave is your Fourth of July? I answer; a day that
reveals to him, more than all other days in the year, the gross
injustice and cruelty to which he is the constant victim. To him,
your celebration is a sham; your boasted liberty, an unholy
license; your national greatness, swelling vanity; your sounds of
rejoicing are empty and heartless; your denunciation of tyrants,
brass-fronted impudence; your shouts of liberty and equality,
hollow mockery; your prayers and hymns, your sermons and
thanksgivings, with all your religious parade and solemnity, are,
to him, more bombast, fraud, deception, impiety, and hypocrisy

—a thin veil to cover up crimes which would disgrace a nation of savages . . ."

"You boast of your love of liberty, your superior civilization, and your pure Christianity . . . You hurl anathemas at the crowned headed tyrants of Russia and Austria and pride yourselves on your Democratic institutions, while you yourselves consent to be the mere *tools* and *bodyguards* of the tyrants of Virginia and Carolina. You invite to your shores fugitives of oppression from abroad, honor them with banquets, greet them with ovations, cheer them, toast them, salute them, protect them, and pour out your money to them like water; but the fugitives from your own land you advertise, hunt, arrest, shoot, and kill. You glory in your refinement and your universal education; yet you maintain a system as barbarous and dreadful as ever stained the character of a nation—a system begun in avarice, supported in pride, and perpetuated in cruelty. You shed tears over fallen Hungary, and make the sad story of her wrongs the theme of your poets, statesmen, and orators, till your gallant sons are ready to fly to arms to vindicate her cause against the oppressor; but, in regard to the ten thousand wrongs of the American slave, you would enforce the strictest silence, and would hail him as an enemy of the nation who dares to make these wrongs the subject of public discourse!"

Douglass dared to make "the ten thousand wrongs" the subject of public discourse. Week after week, year after year, in the crucial decades before the Civil War, he went up and down the North, warning, preaching, demanding. He and other black abolitionists played a major role in shaping the crisis which led to the Civil War.

Like Denmark Vesey, like Martin Luther King, Douglass was a curious blend of idealism and practicality. Nothing indicates this more clearly than his confrontation with John Brown on the eve of the Harpers Ferry Raid. John Brown begged Douglass to accompany him, but Douglass refused, saying the raid was impractical and doomed to failure.

After long arguments, after weeping and much gnashing of teeth, the two men parted, never to meet again, Douglass going toward life, Brown toward death, both men serving in their different ways both life and man. By this, we must understand, as playwright Barry Stavis has said, that two men, both dedicated to the same cause at the same time, can take totally different courses and yet serve in their different ways both history and man.

During the Civil War, Douglass prodded the famous "Slow Coach at Washington" — Abraham Lincoln. Long before Lincoln perceived it, Douglass was saying that the war was a struggle to give America a new birth of freedom. Long before Lincoln saw it, Douglass was saying that the black man was inextricably involved in the root cause of the war and that the war could not be fought or ended without coming to grips with the meaning of the black man and the meaning of America.

Douglass saw the Civil War as a struggle to complete the American Revolution. Legal emancipation alone, he said, would not free the slaves. It would be necessary to train new leaders, reknit shattered Afro-American family life, and instill in the hearts of Southerners respect for democratic processes. The task before America, Douglass said, was "nothing less than radical revolution in all the modes of thought which had flourished under the blighted slave system." The great black abolitionist was openly contemptuous of men like Lincoln who placed the Union above freedom. The old Union, he said, was dead, "We are fighting for something incomparably better than the old Union. We are fighting for unity. Unity of idea, unity of senti-ment, unity of object, unity of institutions, in which there shall be no North, no South, no East, no West, no black, no white, but a solidarity of the nation, making every slave free, and every free man a voter." There was poetry in this audacious conception and Douglass pushed it for all it was worth. With Wendell Phillips and Charles Sumner and Thad Stevens, Douglass prepared the high ground of emancipation which Lincoln occupied so reluctantly and so grudgingly.

After the Emancipation Proclamation was issued, Douglass demanded ballots for the freedmen, and land—and said, with impeccable logic, that "as one learns to swim by swimming, the Negro must learn to vote by voting." Four things, he said, were necessary: "the right to the cartridge box, the ballot box, the jury box"—and "the knowledge box." When the North reneged on its promise and turned the freedmen over to the tender mercies of their former masters, Douglass was merciless in his denunciation. In 1883, he denounced the Afro-Americans' "so-called emancipation as a stupendous fraud, a fraud upon him, a fraud upon the world." America had abandoned the Negro, ignored his rights and left him "a deserted, a defrauded, a swindled, and an outcast man—in law, free; in fact, a slave."

In speech after speech Douglass told America that it was courting social disaster. It was impossible, he said, to degrade black people without degrading the social fabric of America. The perversion of legal processes, he said, would eventually force black people outside the community, for "where justice is denied, where poverty is enforced, where ignorance prevails, and where any one class is made to feel that society is an organized conspiracy to oppress, rob, and degrade...neither persons nor property will be safe..."

"Hungry men," he said, "will eat. Desperate men will commit crime. Outraged men will seek revenge."

Pointing to the summers of 1968 and 1969, Douglass said in 1894 and 1895, that America, if it did not alter its course, would create an aggrieved class of black rebels. And he added significantly: "We want no black Ireland in America."

All this was true and extremely enlightening. But what was to be done? Douglass said black people should refurbish their weapons, dig trenches, expose, warn, appeal, exhort—and contest every inch of ground. Time, he said, would fight the black man's battles — time and the black man's birthrate. "Every year adds to the black man's numbers. Every year adds to his wealth and to his intelligence. These will speak for him."

In these years, Douglass was a magnet, a pole star and a lighthouse. Men said he was waging a hopeless battle, that black people could not win by agitation, litigation, or any other tactic. Perhaps. But they are cowards who fight only when victory is sure. Men, though outnumbered, fight when they reach the wall, when to say no is to affirm one's humanity.

Consider, for example, the range and the depth of Douglass' utterances in this period

The Negro is now discussed on every hand. The platform, the pulpit, the press, and the legislative hall regard him, and struggle with him, as a great and difficult problem, one that requires almost divine wisdom to solve. Men are praying over it. It is always a dangerous symptom when men pray to know what is their duty.

— *Speech, Washington, D.C. 1889*

In whatever else the Negro may have been a failure, he has, in one respect, been a marked and brilliant success. He has managed by one means or another to make himself one of the most prominent and interesting figures that now attract and hold the attention of the world. Go where you will, you will meet him. He is alike present in the study of the learned and thoughtful, and in the play house of the gay and thoughtless. We see him pictured at our street corners, and hear him in the songs of our market places. The low and the vulgar curse him, the snob and the flunky affect to despise him; the mean and the cowardly assault him, because they know that his friends are few, and that they can abuse him with impunity, and with the applause of the coarse and brutal crowd. But, despite it all, the Negro remains like iron or granite, cool, strong, imperturbable and cheerful.

— *Speech, Washington, 1883*

My friends, the present is a critical moment for the colored people of this country; our fate for weal or for woe . . . trembles now in the balance. No man can tell which way the scales will turn. There is not a breeze that sweeps to us from the South, but comes laden with the wail of our suffering people. [This is an hour] when the American people are once more being urged to do from necessity what they should have done from a sense of right, and of sound statesmanship. It is the same old posture of affairs, wherein our rulers do wrong from choice and right from necessity.

—Speech, Washington, 1885

If [federal officials] can protect the rights of white men, they can protect the rights of black men; if they can defend the rights of American citizens abroad, they can defend them at home; if they can use the army to protect the rights of Chinamen, they can use the army to protect the rights of colored men. The only trouble is the will! the will! the will! Here, as elsewhere, "Where there is a will there is a way."

—Speech, Washington, 1886

We warn the American people, and the American government to be wise in their day and generation. The time may come that these whom they now despise and hate, may be needed. These compelled foes may, by and by, be wanted as friends. America cannot always sit, as a queen, in peace and repose. Prouder and stronger governments than hers have been shattered by the bolts of the wrath of a just God. We beseech her to have a care how she goads the sable oppressed in the land. We warn her in the name of retribution, to look to her ways....

—The North Star, 1849

The presence of [deprived citizens] in any section of this country, constituting an aggrieved class, smarting under terrible wrongs, denied the exercise of the commonest rights of humanity, and regarded by the ruling class of that section as outside of the government, outside of the law, outside of society, having nothing in common with the people with whom they live, the sport of mob violence and murder, is not only a disgrace and scandal to that particular section, but a menace to the peace and security of the whole country.

—Pamphlet, 1894

Fellow-citizens! We want no black Ireland in America. We want no aggrieved class in America. Strong as we are without the Negro, we are stronger with him than without him. The power and friendship of seven millions of people scattered all over the country, however humble, are not to be despised.... Our legislators, our Presidents, and our judges should have a care, lest, by forcing these people outside of law, they destroy that

love of country which is needful to the Nation's defense in the day of trouble.
—Speech, Washington, 1883

... let us have peace, but let us have liberty, law and justice first. Let us have the Constitution, with its Thirteenth, Fourteenth, and Fifteenth amendments, fairly interpreted, faithfully executed and cheerfully obeyed in the fullness of their spirit and the completeness of their letter ... When the supreme law of the land is practically set at naught, when humanity is insulted and the rights of the weak are trampled in the dust by a lawless power; when society is divided into two classes, as oppressed and oppressor, there is no power and there can be no power, while the instincts of humanity remain as they are, which can provide solid peace.
—Speech, New York City, 1878

What Abraham Lincoln said in respect of the United States is as true of the colored people as of the relations of these States. They cannot remain half slave and half free. You must give them all or take from them all. Until this half-and-half condition is ended, there will be just ground of complaint. You will have an aggrieved class, and this discussion will go on. Until the public schools shall cease to be caste schools in every part of our country, this discussion will go on. Until the colored man's pathway to the American ballot box, North and South, shall be as smooth and as safe as the same is for the white citizen, this discussion will go on. Until the colored man's right to practice at the bar of our courts, and sit on juries, shall be the universal law and practice of the land, this discussion will go on. Until the courts of the country shall grant the colored man a fair trial and a just verdict, this discussion will go on. Until color shall cease to be a bar to equal participation in the offices and honors of the country, this discussion will go on. Until the trades-unions and the workshops of the country shall cease to proscribe the colored man and prevent his children from learning useful trades, this discussion will go on. Until the American people shall make character, and not color, the criterion of respectability, this discussion will go on. ... In a word, until truth and humanity shall cease to be living ideas, and mankind shall sink back into moral darkness, and the world shall put evil for good, bitter for sweet, and darkness for light, this discussion will go on. Until all humane ideas and civilization shall be banished from the world, this discussion will go on."
—Speech, Washington, 1883

In this period, Douglass — despite his denunciation — became an elder statesman. He was named Marshal of the District of Columbia and Minister to Haiti. He moved to a mansion in Anacostia, Washington, D. C. After the death of his first wife, he married a white woman who was a clerk in his office in the District of Columbia. But he continued to press the claims of black people. He had one foot in the grave on the day a young black student came to him and asked: "Mr. Douglass, what shall I do with my life?" The Old Warrior pulled himself up to his full height and his eyes blazed with the fury of his youth as he said:

"Agitate!

"Agitate!

"Agitate!"

On a cold gray day, February 20, 1895, the Great Agitator slumped to the floor in his mansion at Anacostia Heights, Washington, D. C. By nightfall he was dead. The legislatures of several Northern states passed resolutions of regret. The legislature of North Carolina adjourned for the day to mark the death of one of the greatest black men produced in this country. At his funeral in Washington, John Hutchinson sang the abolitionist song his brother Jesse had dedicated to Douglass:

> *I'll be free, I'll be free, and none shall confine*
> *With fetters and chains this spirit of mine;*
> *From my youth I have vowed in God to rely,*
> *And, despite the oppressor, gain freedom or die.*

A few days later, the black people of Americus, Georgia, held a meeting and voted to contribute to a national fund to erect a monument in Douglass' honor. "No people," these maids and laborers and cotton pickers said, "no people who can produce a Douglass need despair." Some fifty-eight years later, Mary Church Terrell, the great woman leader, echoed this sentiment in an *Ebony* magazine article in which she called Frederick

Frederick Douglass

Douglass the greatest of all Americans. Since that time Frederick Douglass has become a central figure of the black liberation struggle, a fact noted by poet Robert E. Hayden, who wrote:

When it is finally ours, this freedom, this liberty, this beautiful
and terrible thing, needful to man as air,
usable as earth; when it belongs at last to our children,
when it is truly instinct, brain matter, diastole, systole,
reflex action; when it is finally won; when it is more
than the gaudy mumbo jumbo of politicians:
this man, this Douglass, this former slave, this Negro
beaten to his knees, exiled, visioning a world
where none is lonely, none hunted, alien,
this man, superb in love and logic, this man
shall be remembered. Oh, not with statues' rhetoric,
not with legends and poems and wreaths of bronze alone,
but with the lives grown out of his life, the lives
fleshing his dream of the beautiful, needful thing.

THE LAST ABOLITIONIST

William Monroe Trotter

Every revolution was first a thought in one man's mind.

RALPH WALDO EMERSON

WILLIAM MONROE TROTTER

WHEN, IN A calmer time, men sit down to write the definitive history of our era, when they dig beneath the surface for the roots of black resistance, when they dig down deep for the soothsayers and prophets who mirrored our times by anticipating our times, it seems likely that they will focus on William Monroe Trotter, a bold and brilliant agitator who is virtually unknown today.

Ignored by a written history which skims the surface and misses the deeper currents underneath, Trotter is nevertheless honored by a living history which has confirmed his prophetic judgments and insights.

A true pioneer, decades ahead of his time, Trotter laid the first stone of the modern protest movement.

It was Trotter who mobilized the forces that checked the triumphant advance of Booker T. Washington's program of accommodation and submission.

It was Trotter who opened a new cycle of struggle by making the first faltering steps in the direction of direct action and mass mobilization.

Looking back on Trotter, thirteen years after his death, William Harrison said in the *Negro History Bulletin* that he was "a figure of national and even international significance and eminence" who made five major contributions:

1. "He startled the nation by challenging Booker T.

Washington at the outset of his career...."

2. "He defied President Woodrow Wilson when the latter instituted segregation of Negroes employed in offices of the Federal Government in Washington."

3. "He threw down the gauntlet against racial discrimination on a world scale when he intervened at the Versailles Peace Conference in 1919...."

4. "He pioneered in the staging of picket lines to protest plays derogatory to the Negro people...."

5. "He was the first American Negro leader to organize mass struggle on issues with national and international significance since the days of Frederick Douglass and the abolitionists."

What makes this record all the more remarkable is that Trotter was a black blueblood. The son of James Monroe Trotter, a leading intellectual and politician, he was born on April 7, 1872. He never knew hunger or want. Nor did he experience the most brutal aspects of blackness in America. He was raised in a posh home in the predominantly white Boston suburb of Hyde Park; he attended the predominantly white Hyde Park schools and moved on with his affluent peers to Harvard University, from which he was graduated in 1895 *magna cum laude*. In 1896 he received an M.A. degree from Harvard. W. E. B. Du Bois was an acquaintance at Harvard, but the two students differed considerably in temperament and orientation. Both were loners, but they were loners in different ways, which is another way of saying that they suffered differently.

After graduating from Harvard with honors and a Phi Beta Kappa key, Trotter married the socially prominent Geraldine Pindell and settled down to a promising career as a real estate broker. There stretched before him then a bright vista of achievement in the echelons of the black elite. But this vision seemed somehow despicable to Trotter, who was haunted by the creeping misery of the black masses. Most members of the black elite believed they could fight racism as individuals by proving that they were clean, rational, and respectable. This orientation, which was based on the one-by-one admission of whitewashed blacks into American society, repelled Trotter, who saw clearly that black people were oppressed collectively and that a collective effort was necessary to destroy this oppression. He was particularly exercised by the Horatio Alger individualism of Booker T. Washington, the anti-protest leader who dominated the headlines of the day.

Looking back on that period later, Trotter said "The conviction grew upon me that pursuit of business, money, civic or literary position was like building a house upon the sands, if race prejudice and persecution and public discrimination for mere color was to spread up from the South and result in a fixed caste of color. I realized that the Democracy which I had enjoyed at dear old Harvard was not secure for Americans of color, just because of their pigmentation. It would mean that, however native and to the manner born, every colored American would be really a civil outcast, forever an alien, in the public life."

"So," Trotter continued, "I plunged in to contend for full equality in all things governmental, political, civil, and judicial, as far as race, creed, or color was concerned. I opposed all compromise, whether advocated by Professor Booker T. Washington or President William Howard Taft, to say nothing of race oppression as advocated by Senator Benjamin Tillman."

With scarcely a backward glance, Trotter repudiated the pretensions of the black elite and embraced a collective vocation of liberation.

Why did Trotter give up the rich red meat of elitehood for the lean fare of agitation?

In other words, why do some men choose the underdogs

when their credentials entitle them to a seat at the table of upperdogs?

The obvious answer is that an unjust world requires, *demands* the sacrifice of the Just. Even more importantly, the friction provided by men like Trotter is necessary for the health of society, which clings tenaciously to the old and the safe. But this view is rejected by many men who seek the causes for the transformation of the Trotters of the world in psychological events—in unhappy childhoods, personal frustrations, and delayed rebellions against remembered fathers.

Like almost all radicals, Trotter was accused of raising hell for the sake of raising hell; he was accused of opposing unjust social policies and interests out of a desire for martyrdom. Proto-Freudians said he lashed out at the environment in an unconscious effort to provoke the punishments and the isolation he desired. But these answers were at worst fatuous and at best ideological justifications for the status quo Trotter rejected. For if personal frustration and unhappy childhood produced radicals, most of the people in the world would be radical.

It would be better perhaps to confront the mystery of men like Trotter by admitting frankly the close connection between the personal and the social, between private troubles and social troubles. This explanation does not exclude personal projects—differences in temperament, sensitivity, and reaction to critical life experiences. But it insists upon the close connection between the man and the situation. And it emphasises the ideological assumptions of the question: Why do some men become radicals? In a world shot through with oppression and injustice, in a world where most people do not have enough to eat, where most people are illiterate and diseased, would it not be more logical to ask: Why aren't all men radicals?

Trotter asked this question at the turn of the century. He couldn't understand why so many black men were silent in the face of so much misery. He couldn't understand why so many educated black men supinely accepted the submissive program of Booker T. Washington. And he decided to trouble the water by shattering the conspiracy of silence the white power structure had imposed on a new generation which was restive under the weight of the powerful Washington machine. Aided by George Forbes, another well-educated member of the Boston elite, Trotter founded the Boston *Guardian* in 1901 and dedicated his life to the destruction of Booker T. Washington and the idea Washington represented. Significantly, Trotter established the *Guardian* on the same floor in the same building which had housed William Lloyd Garrison's *Liberator*. The motto of the Guardian was, "For every right, with all thy might."

Booker T. Washington responded to the Trotter campaign with a ruthlessly efficient campaign of harassment. He tried first to silence Trotter by subsidizing another Boston newspaper and by encouraging costly and time-consuming legal suits. But nothing worked: The Boston Cato went his lonely way, thundering: Booker T. Washington must be destroyed. Worse, he followed Washington from city to city in an unsuccessful attempt to question him about his program of accommodation.

At this juncture, Washington made an extraordinary blunder by accepting an invitation to speak at Columbus Avenue AME Zion Church in the heart of Boston's Trotterland. When he rose to speak on July 30, 1903, the Trotterites were ready. Several of Trotter's supporters, stationed at strategic points in the audience, leaped to their feet and heckled Washington. Trotter himself posed several carefully phrased questions, asking: "In view of the fact that you are understood to be unwilling to insist upon the Negro having his every right (both civil and political) would it not be a calamity at this juncture to make you our leader? Is the rope and the torch all the race is to get under your leadership?

As the heckling continued, the audience became unmanageable, and police were called to restore order. When Washington resumed his speech, he unwisely told an equivocal anecdote about a balky mule and the church heaved with hisses, shouts, and screams. In the confusion someone threw a batch of red pepper, and the crowd panicked, men and women trampling each other in a mindless dash for the nearest exits. When order was restored, Trotter and several of his aides were arrested. Trotter later served a thirty-day sentence at the Charles Street jail.

News reports of the Boston riot startled America—which was, one can suppose, Trotter's objective. It had not been possible up to that point to get full coverage of the anti-Washington viewpoint. Having selected Washington as *the* Negro leader, the white power structure had carefully protected him from the crossfire of black dissidents. But it was impossible to suppress the Boston riot, and word went out that some black people were displeased with "their" leader.

By organizing the Boston riot, Trotter moved the seething ideological dispute in the black community to a new level. He also created an act which made men stand up and take sides, either for or against Booker T. Washington. In the wake of this event, W. E. B. Du Bois abandoned his scholarly detachment and came down hard on the side of the radicals. "While I have not always agreed with Mr. Trotter's methods," Du Bois wrote a friend, "I have had the greatest admiration for his singlehearted earnestness & devotion to a great cause & I am the more minded to express this respect publicly when I see him the object of petty persecution & dishonest attack."

With Trotter and Du Bois in the forefront, the black radicals rallied and organized an anti-Washington front. On July 11, 1905, twenty-nine black professionals met near Niagara Falls and inaugurated the Niagara movement, which marked the beginning of the modern protest movement. In 1906, a larger group met at Harpers Ferry, the site of John Brown's assault on the slave system, and issued an address to the nation. This address, largely written by Trotter and Du Bois, raised issues which are still on the agenda of the Commonwealth:

In detail our demands are clear and unequivocal. First, we would vote; with the right to vote goes everything: Freedom, manhood, the honor of your wives, the chastity of your daughters, the right to work, and the chance to rise, and let no man listen to those who deny this.

We want full manhood suffrage, and we want it now, henceforth and forever.

Second. We want discrimination in public accommodation to cease. Separation in railway and street cars, based simply on race and color, is un-American, undemocratic, and silly. We protest against all such discrimination.

Third. We claim the right of free men to walk, talk, and be with them that wish to be with us. No man has a right to choose another man's friends, and to attempt to do so is an impudent interference with the most fundamental human privilege.

Fourth. We want the laws enforced against rich as well as poor, against Capitalist as well as Laborer; against white as well as black. We are not more lawless than the white race, we are more often arrested, convicted and mobbed. We want justice even for criminals and outlaws. We want the Constitution of the country enforced. We want Congress to take charge of Congressional elections. We want the Fourteenth Amendment carried out to the letter and every State disfranchised which attempts to disfranchise its rightful voters. We want the Fifteenth Amendment enforced and no State allowed to base its franchise simply on color.

The failure of the Republican Party in Congress at the session just closed to redeem its pledge of 1904 with reference to suffrage conditions at the South seems a plain, deliberate, and premeditated breach of promise, and stamps that party as guilty of obtaining votes under false pretense.

Fifth. We want our children educated. The school system in the country districts of the South is a disgrace and in few towns and cities are the Negro schools what they ought to be. We want the national government to step in and wipe out illiteracy in the South. Either the United States will destroy ignorance or ignorance will destroy the United States.

And when we call for education we mean real education. We believe in work. We ourselves are workers, but work is not necessarily education.

Education is the development of power and ideal. We want our children trained as intelligent human beings should be, and we will fight for all time against any proposal to educate black boys and girls simply as servants and underlings, or simply for the use of other people. They have a right to know, to think, to aspire.

These are some of the chief things which we want. How shall we get them? By voting where we may vote, by persistent, unceasing agitation, by hammering at the truth, by sacrifice and work.

In a pioneering effort to give thrust to these words, Trotter and Du Bois put together an NAACP-type structure based on litigation, education, research. From the beginning, this organization was hampered by its narrow base (it was composed primarily of black intellectuals) and by internal dissension. Neither Trotter nor Du Bois was an organization man, and the presence of both in a single organization made strife inevitable. Trotter finally withdrew from the group and established his own organization, the National Equal Rights League. At that point, Trotter and Du Bois disagreed on several issues. Trotter placed more stress on independent black political action. He also championed racially autonomous organizations.

When, in 1909, the dwindling Niagara militants and white liberals organized the National Association for the Advancement of Colored People, Trotter, true to his principles, refused to join. In his view, the NAACP was too little, too late, and too white.

Trotter's refusal to link up with NAACP forces marked the fundamental turning point in his life. From that point onward he was overshadowed by Du Bois and NAACP-oriented leaders. But for all that he remained a force to be reckoned with. As the leader of the National Equal Rights League, he continued to denounce compromisers of the left and the right. On one celebrated occasion, he stormed into the White House and denounced Woodrow Wilson, who was segregating toilets and office facilities in Washington, D.C. According to participants, the Harvard-trained black rebel and the former president of Princeton had an acrimonious, jaw-to-jaw confrontation.

Trotter opened a new front during World War I by linking the Afro-American's struggle with the cause of the colonized peoples of Africa and Asia. When the government refused to give him a passport to attend the Paris Peace Conference, he disguised himself as a cook and sailed on a second-class steamer. In Paris, he peppered the delegates with pleas and admonitions. The conferees turned a deaf ear to these pleas and wrote a for-whites-only peace treaty.

Returning to America, Trotter redoubled his efforts in the field of agitation. In 1922, 1923, 1924, and 1926, he led delegations to the White House. In the same period, he experimented with direct action techniques by leading picket lines and demonstrations against the movie, *The Birth of a Nation.* In his paper, he defended the Scottsboro Boys and New Deal economic policies. He also continued to press his favorite project, "Crispus Attucks Day."

In a wiser world, Trotter's story would have had a happier ending. But history is tricky. It does not always reward the first pioneer; nor does it always remember. Sometimes, as in the case of Trotter, History pushes a valiant man into the briar bush of the new in order to prepare the way for a successor who has fewer thistles to contend with and reaps a larger immediate return.

Did Trotter perceive this?

Did he think of these things as the world turned from him and as others reaped the plaudits of the crowd?

No one knows. He was not a whining man; he asked no quarter and gave none. Until the end, he walked his lonely way, raising alarums and jousting with enemies, real and imagined.

Toward the end, he was, it seems, a trifle disoriented and disheartened. But he brightened up appreciably on his sixty-second birthday—April 7, 1934. That night, after dinner, he took a stroll, as was his wont, on the roof of his Boston boarding house. Some time before dawn, he walked again on the roof and toppled to his death.

However he came to his end, whether by accident or suicide, Trotter's life was a parable of sacrifice and selflessness in the service of a cause which has gained more from great failures than from petty triumphs.

Was Trotter then a failure?

Some men said so without realizing that there are magnificent failures greater than anything the world calls success. No man fails who chooses failure when what the world calls success can only be had at the price of manhood. No man fails who falls in the front ranks of battle, facing the enemy.

In the end, it might be said of Trotter that he was a dialogue History carried on with itself. In him and through him, History clarified itself and moved to another level. And men today who never heard Trotter's name are his debtors and his disciples.

BLACK RENAISSANCE

Marcus Garvey

*Up you mighty race, you can accomplish
what you will.*

MARCUS GARVEY

MARCUS GARVEY

MARCUS MOZIAH GARVEY was born in Jamaica and died in London. Although he lived fifty-three turbulent years, he only spent ten years in the United States of America. But during that ten-year span he played a role of power in this land no black man has surpassed and few black men have matched.

Garvey was an agitator-organizer, perhaps the best one produced in black America.

His doctrine was black nationalism.

His message was racial pride and regeneration.

His motto was "Africa for the Africans, at home and abroad."

Although he was not the first black nationalist leader, he carried the insights of the pre-Civil War nationalists to new and dazzling heights. In the twenties, some forty years before Malcolm X reached his peak, Garvey organized the largest black mass movement in the history of America and collected more money (an estimated ten million dollars in one two-year period) than any black leader before him or after him. In the process, he permanently altered the consciousness of the black men of America and Africa and the islands of the sea.

No one could have predicted that blackness would carry Garvey to such heights when he was born on August 17, 1887, in St. Ann's Bay on the northern coast of Jamaica. The youngest of eleven children born to Marcus and Sarah Garvey, he grew up in a relatively inarticulate environment dominated by British colonialism. He attended local schools and later moved to Kingston, where he mastered the trade of printing. By the age of twenty, he was master printer and foreman of one of the largest firms on the island. He later participated in a local strike and was blacklisted by Jamaican firms. After an unsuccessful venture as an editor, he began a period of migration, drifting from Costa Rica to Panama to London.

In London, in the midst of World War I, Garvey came across a copy of *Up From Slavery*. "I read *Up From Slavery* by Booker T. Washington," he said, "and then my doom—if I may so call it—of being a race leader dawned upon me.... I asked: 'Where is the black man's government? Where is his king and his kingdom? Where is his President, his country, and his ambassador, his army, his navy, his men of big affairs?' I could not find them, and then I declared, 'I will help to make them.' " In one of the little ironies for which history is famous, Booker T. Washington, the advocate of submission and accommodation to the status quo, sowed the seeds of a defiant black nationalism which would lead to Elijah Muhammad, Malcolm X, and the Black Power advocates of the midcentury.

Garvey returned to Jamaica "determined that the black man would not continue to be kicked about by all the other races and nations of the world...." He had a new vision of "a new world of black men, not peons, serfs, dogs and slaves, but a nation of sturdy men making their impress upon civilization and causing a new light to dawn upon the human race." He said his brain "was afire" with the possibility of "uniting all the Negro peoples of the world into one great body to establish a country and a Government absolutely their own."

On August 1, 1914, Garvey established his structural foundation—the Universal Negro Improvement Association (UNIA). According to a manifesto issued on this date, the new organization was designed to rehabilitate black men and promote "a Universal Confraternity among the race."

The response to Garvey's projected crusade was something less than overwhelming in Jamaica. "I was openly hated and persecuted," Garvey said, "by some of these colored men of the island who did not want to be classified as Negroes but as white."

Rebuffed at home, Garvey decided to begin his crusade in America. And on March 23, 1916, he arrived in the Harlem of the New World. He was twenty-eight at the time—short, black, with a dandyish moustache and piercing, magnetic eyes. Years of reading, traveling, and organizing had sharpened his skills. He knew what to do with a crowd; and he was a master of the gifts that prevail in organizational power plays.

Garvey was ready for Harlem; and Harlem was ready for Garvey.

Tension had been building in the black communities of America for several years, and millions of black people were swarming to Harlem and other Northern centers in an unprecedented mass migration. The new migrants soon discovered that Harlem was not the promised land. In addition to the "normal" manifestations of racism, there were the new and explosive forces released by the war. One reflection of the new white mood was a resurgence of the Klan in Indiana and other Northern states. Another reflection of the same anxiety and fear was the Red Summer of 1919, a summer of twenty-six race riots and massacres.

This situation was made to order for Marcus Garvey, who rolled up his sleeves and went to work. On street corners and in small halls, he preached a new racial message of black consciousness and self-determination. "When Europe was inhabited by a race of cannibals," he said, "a race of savages, naked men, heathens and pagans, Africa was peopled with a race of cultured black men, who were masters in art, science and literature; men who were cultured and refined; men who, it was said, were like gods. . . . Why, then, should we lose hope? Black men, you were once great; you shall be great again. Lose not courage, lose not faith, go forward...."

Garvey denounced the programs and policies of the traditional Negro organizations, saying that American racism was too deep and pervasive to be eradicated by prayers, petitions, and litigation. Garvey admitted that the demands of civil rights leaders were just. "But the great white majority," he added, "will not grant them, and thus we march on to danger."

What was the solution?

Power, Garvey said. "If we must have justice," he said, "we must be strong; if we must be strong, we must come together; if we must come together, we can only do so through a system of organization." He added: "Don't be deceived, there is no justice but strength. In other words, might is right; and if you must be heard and respected you will have to accumulate nationally in Africa those resources that will compel unjust men to think twice before they act."

Power in America, Garvey said, was a peripheral and transitional goal. The ultimate solution was a return to Africa. Like Herzl, the founder of Zionism, Garvey said that minorities would never be respected anywhere until they had established a strong and independent state of their own.

While waiting for the improbable transfer of black people in Africa, Garvey pressed a shrewd and psychologically sound program of demystification. He went to the heart of the problem by ripping away the shame and inferiority feelings which were stunting the growth of black men. He glorified everything black, gave Jesus and Mary sun-tans, and established his own African Orthodox Church.

Garvey's program electrified black America. Within two years, the UNIA was one of the largest black organizations in the ghetto; and the organization's paper, the *Negro World*, had a circulation of from sixty to two hundred thousand. By 1923, Garvey claimed a total of six million followers. But his critics said the organization only had a "nominal" membership of about one hundred thousand.

Garvey gave his followers parades, uniforms, pageantry. For women, there was the Black Cross Nurse organization. For men, there was the African Legion with dark blue uniforms and red trousers. For men, women, and children, there were Liberty Halls from one end of the country to the other. A new flag flew in these halls. It was red (for the blood of the race), black (for the color of the race), and green (for the hope of the race).

There was more than theatrics in the Garvey movement. Garvey and his aides organized a chain of cooperative grocery stores, restaurants, factories, publishing houses, and factories. They also organized the celebrated Black Star Steamship Line.

The Garvey movement peaked in 1920 with an international convention which drew 25,000 persons to Madison Square Garden. During this convention, Garvey declared himself provisional president of the African Republic. In a speech to the convention, he said:

"The Negroes of the world say, 'We are striking homewards towards Africa to make the big black republic.' And in the making of Africa a big black republic, what is the barrier? The barrier is the white man; and we say to the white man who now dominates Africa that it is to his interest to clear out of Africa now, because we are coming not as in the time of Father Abraham, 200,000 strong, but we are coming 400,000,000 strong, and we mean to retake every square inch of the 12,000,000 square miles of African territory belonging to us by right Divine.... We are out to get what has belonged to us politically, socially, economically, and in every way."

Like all men, Garvey had his faults. He was vain, autocratic, bombastic. And these negative qualities, together with the pressures generated by black and white enemies, led him into a series of errors which doomed his venture. In 1925, he was convicted of using the mail to defraud in a complicated scheme to finance his steamship company. After two years of imprisonment in the federal penitentiary, he said: "Be assured that I planted well the seed of Negro or black nationalism which cannot be destroyed even by the foul play that has been meted out to me." He added:

"When I am dead wrap the mantle of the Red, Black, and Green around me, for in the new life I shall rise with God's grace and blessing to lead the millions up the heights of triumphs with the colors that you well know. Look for me in the whirlwind of the storm, look for me all around you, for, with God's grace, I shall come and bring with me countless millions of black slaves who have died in America and the West Indies and the millions in Africa to aid you in the fight for Liberty, Freedom, and Life."

In 1940, his dream shattered, Marcus Garvey died in London, without having set foot on the land of Mother Africa. "That," commented Professor Albert Bushnell Hart, "is the difference between success and failure. Had Garvey succeeded in his undertakings he would have been uncontestably the greatest figure of the twentieth century. Having failed, he is considered a fool."

It must be added, however, that the difference between success and failure in ventures of this kind is small indeed. Garvey left behind living monuments and is considered the prophet of black consciousness and African nationalism by the black nationalists of America and the leaders of the emerging states of Africa.

DUSK *of* DAWN

W. E. B. Du Bois

The problem of the twentieth century is the problem of the color line — the relation of the darker to the lighter races of men in Asia and Africa, in America and the islands of the sea.

W. E. B. DU BOIS

W. E. B. DU BOIS

ON THURSDAY NIGHT, February 23, 1893, a young black student performed an extraordinary ceremony in a small room in Berlin.

He was alone in the room. No one knew what he was doing or why. No one knew then that it would be important later — no one, that is, except the black student who answered to the name of William Edward Burghardt Du Bois.

A solitary black pebble on the hot white sand of Berlin, a cultural pinnacle of triumphant Western civilization, Du Bois was completing a graduate course at the University of Berlin. The prospects before him were not promising. He was an orphan, he was poor, and he had more pride than could be profitably used. Most important of all, he was black, and this was an age of unbridled racism. In that year, in the heyday of Victoria and Leopold and "Pitchfork" Ben Tillman, the white man bestrode the earth like a colossus and the future was white with the promise of endless Western expansion. No one knew then that Western civilization was about to unravel at the seams. No one knew then that the bubble was about to burst — no one, that is, except W. E. B. Du Bois, who celebrated his twenty-fifth birthday on that faraway night by vowing to become the Moses of the black people of Africa and America. To seal that vow, he improvised a ritual of regeneration, using Greek wine, candles, oil, and oranges. In the stillness of the small room, he prayed, sang, "cried &c." Then he made "a sacrifice to the *Zeitgeist* of Work, God, and Mercy." Later that night, before closing his eyes, W. E. B. Du Bois wrote strange words in his diary:

> I am glad I am living. I rejoice as a strong man to run a race, and I am strong—is it egotism is it assurance—or is it the silent call of the world spirit that makes me feel that I am royal and that beneath my sceptre a world of kings shall bow? The hot dark blood of that black forefather born king of men— is beating at my heart, and I know that I am either a genius or a fool.
>
> I wonder what I am—I wonder what the world is—I wonder if life is worth the striving. I do not know—perhaps I shall never know; but this I do know: be the Truth what it may I shall seek it on the pure assumption that it is worth seeking—and Heaven nor Hell, God nor Devil shall turn me from my purpose till I die....
>
> I am striving to make my life all that life may be—and I am limiting that strife only in so far as that strife is incompatible with others of my brothers and sisters making their lives similar. The crucial question now is where this limit comes ... God knows I am sorely puzzled ... I therefore take the work that the Unknown lays in my hands & work for the rise of the Negro people, taking for granted that their best development means the best development in the world.
>
> This night before my life's altar I reiterate, what my heart has—

The tumbling flow of words breaks off here and resumes with this promise:

> These are my plans: to make a name in science, to make a name in literature and thus to raise my race. Or perhaps to raise a visible empire in Africa thro' England, France, or Germany.
>
> I wonder what will be the outcome? Who knows?
>
> I will go unto the King—which is not according to the law & if I perish— I *perish*.

When, seventy years later, W. E. B. Du Bois perished, having gone up to the King, in spite of and in defiance of law, he had made a name in science and in literature and had lifted his race by founding the modern black protest movement and the Pan-African movement. In Africa, at his death, there was a "visible empire"; and, in America, there were two visible monuments—

the NAACP, which he helped to found in 1909, and the Freedom movement, which is the reverberating echo of the new ideas he articulated between 1903 and 1933.

But in death, as in life, Du Bois is a figure of controversy. On the edge of the grave, disillusioned and disheartened, he made two decisions that will doubtless exercise future historians. In 1961, at the age of ninety-three, he became a member of the Communist party. Two years later, shortly before his ninety-fifth birthday, he became a citizen of Ghana. Some Americans contend that "overzealous" defenders of the status quo hounded Du Bois out of America and into the Communist party. However, he came to his ordeal, his life — particularly the last period — was a bitter parable of a bitter time.

Parables apart, this fact remains. Du Bois was a mountain no Afro-American, or white man, for that matter, can ignore. It can be said, in fact, that no one can understand the Afro-American who does not understand the early Du Bois.

In 1934, the Board of Directors of the NAACP said: "... the ideas which he propounded [in the *Crisis*] and in his books and essays transformed the Negro world as well as a large portion of the liberal white world, so that the whole problem of the relation of black and white races has ever since had a completely new orientation. He created, what never existed before, a Negro intelligentsia, and many who have never read a word of his writings are his spiritual disciples and descendants. Without him the Association could never have been what it was and is."

Du Bois, who cared nothing for convention and always spoke the Truth (his capital) as he saw it, agreed.

"I think I may say without boasting," he wrote, "that in the period from 1910 to 1930 I was a main factor in revolutionizing the attitude of the American Negro toward caste. My stinging hammer blows made Negroes aware of themselves, confident of their possibilities and determined in self-assertion. So much so that today common slogans among the Negro people are taken bodily from the words of my mouth."

Who was this man who spoke with such immodesty, such eloquence — and such truth?

Almost despite himself, Du Bois was the Columbus of the Negro's New World. An intellectual giant, probably the largest mind produced in black America, an actionist, a seer, a prophet, he discovered the shores beyond the Europeanized West. He was perhaps the first black man to say with all his heart and all his soul that the world did not belong to white people. He was perhaps the first black man to say in action that God had placed the Negro in the midst of Western civilization to civilize it. *Negritude*, the African personality, protest, Africa for Africans, the sociology of the slums, *The Gifts of Black Folk*, *The Souls of Black Folk*, the sorrow songs: all found a place in the world view of the prophet who said in 1903: "The problem of the twentieth century is the problem of the color line — the relation of the darker to the lighter races of men in Asia and Africa, in America and the islands of the sea."

Du Bois was a product of the rising tide of color he symbolized. He was one month old when Grant became President, eight years old when Victoria became Empress of India, nine when white men with guns nullified Reconstruction and the Fourteenth and Fifteenth amendments, sixty-two when Gandhi marched to the sea, and ninety-five when he died on the eve of the March on Washington.

Born February 23, 1868, in the shadow of slavery, Du Bois was the son of Alfred and Mary Du Bois, two members of the small free black elite in the town of Great Barrington in western Massachusetts. There was in his veins, he said, "a flood of Negro blood, a strain of French, a bit of Dutch, but, thank God, no Anglo-Saxon." Du Bois grew up with a strong sense of family and place. The Du Boises were poor but proud and they tended, Du Bois recalled later, to look down on the poor white immigrants who composed the bulk of the working class of

W. E. B. Du Bois

Great Barrington.

Du Bois spent the first seventeen years of his life in this climate of genteel poverty. His father died while he was quite young and his mother died soon after he finished high school. As a result, the future leader spent part of his early life as the ward of relatives.

Despite his vulnerable position, Du Bois decided quite early that he was destined for big things. How he learned this is a mystery, but we catch him at the age of fifteen in an extraordinary and, considering the circumstances, somewhat immodest pursuit: collecting and annotating his papers for posterity.

Small-boned, intense, pugnacious, Du Bois made an excellent record at the predominantly white Great Barrington public schools. Although there was little overt racism in Great Barrington, he perceived early that he was beyond the pale and he reacted with the cold fury that would characterize his later life. He has written that "the sky was bluest when I could beat my mates at examination-time, or beat them at a foot-race, or even beat their stringy heads."

With the help of a church scholarship, Du Bois went in the fall of 1885 to Fisk University in Nashville, Tennessee. This was the first of several turning points in his life. He had never really known black people before. Now suddenly he was plunged into "the whole gorgeous color gamut of the American Negro world...." Du Bois said later that his first day on the Fisk campus was something of a religious experience. He wandered, exhilarated, across the campus, sampling the colors— "bronze, mahogany, coffee, gold." At the first dinner at Fisk, he sat opposite a girl "of whom I have often said, no human being could possibly have been as beautiful as she seemed to my eyes that far-off September night of 1885." Ever afterwards, Du Bois would be fascinated by the beauty of black skin color and astonished by the inability of white Americans to perceive that beauty.

After graduation from Fisk, Du Bois moved on to Harvard, where he repeated part of his college work and earned M.A. and Ph.D. degrees in history. His Ph.D. dissertation, the first of nineteen works of non-fiction and fiction, was entitled *The Suppression of the African Slave Trade*. Du Bois later received a scholarship from the Slater Fund and went off for two additional years of study at the University of Berlin.

There are men in every group who will accept life on no other basis except absolute equality, men who present the hardness of their spirit to the hardness of the world, asking no favors and giving none. Du Bois was such a man. He expected, anticipated, even provoked, the hostile consciousness of the white Other; and one can imagine him smiling disdainfully when the hostility came. He had, he said, "an island within." He was Du Bois — he needed no one.

The two years in Europe changed Du Bois' perspective. His human contacts, both at the university and in European cities, were singularly free of the collective contempt he experienced in America. He went sailing on the Rhine with a German family and spent happy holidays with French, English, and German boys and girls. When a fraulein, "blue-eyed Dora," confessed her readiness to marry him "*gleich!*" Du Bois told her "frankly and gravely" that it would be unfair to himself and cruel to her for a colored man to take a white bride to America."

As a result of his experiences in Europe, Du Bois developed a more complex view of life and race. "I became more human," he said, "[and] learned the place in life of 'Wine, Women, and Song'; I ceased to hate or suspect people simply because they belonged to one race or color...."

In July, 1894, having dedicated himself to the liberation of colored peoples, Du Bois returned to America and began his academic career at Wilberforce, where he taught Latin and Greek for two years and met Nina Gomer, "the slender, quiet and dark-eyed girl who became Mrs. Du Bois in 1896." That same year, 1896, he went to the University of Pennsylvania and made the first in-depth study of an urban Negro community, *The Philadelphia Negro*. The next year, 1897, he entered on his "life plan" as a professor of economics and history at Atlanta University, where he organized a series of annual conferences on the urban Negro, and produced a series of studies that gave a new orientation to the Negro situation in America.

At this point, Du Bois was at the height of his considerable powers. Trim, agile, with chiseled features and a Van Dyke beard, Du Bois presented a picture of fastidious determination. He was seldom seen without the cane and gloves of a German student. "I doubtless strutted," he said, "and I certainly knew what I wanted. My redeeming features were infinite capacity for work, and terrible earnestness, with appalling and tactless frankness."

Although Du Bois was probably the best-educated and most gifted scholar in Atlanta, he was proscribed as a pariah. Because of the humiliation that awaited him off-campus, Du Bois lived as though the city of Atlanta did not exist. He never rode a streetcar, never entered a movie or a concert hall.

While the Du Boises were living in Atlanta, a son, Burghardt, and a daughter, Yolanda, were born to them. The girl survived but Burghardt, the first-born, died eighteen months after birth. In a house still ringing with the cries of a bereaved mother, Du Bois sat down and wrote the most searing essay in the history of race relations. In this essay, "On the Passing of the First Born," Du Bois expressed an "awful gladness" that his son had "escaped" the horrors of living the life of a black male in America. Many years later, a young man attempted to read this essay aloud. He stumbled along until he came to the words "awful gladness." Then, sobbing, he flung the book across the room and said: "No man has a right to utter such terrible sorrow."

He died at eventide, when the sun lay like a brooding sorrow above the western hills, veiling its face; when the winds spoke not, and the trees, the great green trees he loved, stood motionless. . . .

We could not lay him in the ground there in Georgia, for the earth there is strangely red; so we bore him away to the northward, with his flowers and his little folded hands. In vain, in vain! — for where, O God! beneath thy broad blue sky shall my dark baby rest in peace, — where Reverence dwells, and Goodness, and a freedom that is free?

All that day and all that night there sat an awful gladness in my heart, — nay, blame me not if I see the world thus darkly through the Veil, and my soul whispers ever to me, saying, "not dead, not dead, but escaped, not bond, but free." No bitter meanness now shall sicken his baby heart till it die a living death. . . .

By the turn of the century, events in Atlanta and in the outer world had changed Du Bois' mind about the nature of racial reality. He recalled later that there were five lynchings a week during this period and "each death was a scar on my soul." The depth of Du Bois' emerging despair can be gauged by his passionate arraignment of God in the *Litany* he wrote after the brutal Atlanta riots of 1906.

Doth not his justice of hell stink in Thy nostrils, O God. How long shall the mounting flood of innocent blood roar in Thine ears and pound on our hearts for vengeance? Pile the pale frenzy of blood-crazed brutes, who do such deeds, high on Thine Altar, Jehoveh Jireh, and burn it in hell forever and forever!

Forgive us, good Lord; we know not what we say!

Bewildered we are and passion-tossed, mad with the madness of a mobbed and mocked and murdered people; staring at the armposts of Thy Throne, we raise our shackled hands and charge Thee, God, by the bones of our stolen fathers, by the tears of our dead mothers, by the very blood of Thy Crucified Christ: what meaneth this? Tell us the plan; give us the sign!

Keep not thou silent, O God!

Sit not longer dumb, Lord God, deaf to our prayers and dumb to our dumb suffering. Surely, Thou, too, are not white, O Lord, a pale, bloodless, heartless thing!

Du Bois' efforts as a poet and professor were based on a belief that racism was caused by ignorance. His remedy then was Truth. As the years wore on and as outrage piled on outrage, Du Bois came to see that the old saw, "The truth will set you free," is only true in the very, very long run. For Du Bois, analysis was always a step toward or away from action. Having decided that the truth was not enough, he descended from his ivory tower and tried "with bare hands to lift the earth."

Beginning in 1903 with the publication of his book, *The Souls of Black Folk*, a group of essays that had an impact on its age not unlike that of James Baldwin's *The Fire Next Time* sixty years later, Du Bois began to attack the program and policies of Booker T. Washington. To Washington's program of accommodation and submission, Du Bois opposed a program of "ceaseless agitation and insistent demands for equality," involving "the use of force of every sort: moral suasion, propaganda and . . . even physical resistance." To Washington's philosophy of "individual education," Du Bois opposed a program of higher education with special emphasis on the Talented Tenth, an elite group which would lead, inspire, exalt, serve, and guide the masses.

Taking the offensive two years later, Du Bois helped organize the germinal Niagara movement, an NAACP-like organization composed of black professionals and intellectuals. Although this group made few concrete gains, it prepared the way for the NAACP and educated black people in a strategy of protest and litigation. Du Bois and the Niagara cadre played a pivotal role in the organization of the NAACP, which merged the forces of black militancy and white liberalism in 1909. In 1910, Du Bois, then forty-two, resigned from Atlanta University and became director of publications of the new organization and editor of its organ, the *Crisis*. As *Crisis* editor, Du Bois set the tone for organization and educated a whole generation of black people in the art of protest. Many people in fact believed Du Bois and the *Crisis* were the NAACP, a belief Du Bois did nothing to dispel. By 1918, William Edward Burghardt Du Bois was by far the most prominent black man in all America.

Du Bois was not a natural leader. He despised, he said, "the essential demagoguery" of personal leadership. He could not "slap people on the back and make friends of strangers. I could not easily break down an inherited reserve; or at all times curb a biting, critical tongue." As a result, Du Bois won influence, not power. His, as he said, was a leadership solely of ideas.

Du Bois' life style caused considerable tension at the NAACP, where he operated the *Crisis* as a personal fief and reserved the right to criticize the Association in its own journal. Another source of conflict was Du Bois' racial program which differed considerably from the program of the Association. Du Bois, for example, championed what he called "economic democracy." He was also an exponent of what is now called *Negritude*. Negroes, he said, had a special mission in the world. What he envisioned was a "new and great Negro ethos." To create this ethos, Negroes, he said, had to channel their power—physical, political, economic, and spiritual—through the whole Negro group. What was required, he said in a 1915 article, was "conscious self-realization and self-direction." The NAACP was essential in this effort, he said. But larger black control was necessary. "We must not only support but control this and similar organizations and hold them unswervingly to our objects, and our ideals."

World War I, which Du Bois called "the climacteric of my pilgrimage," created a new Du Bois with a "vaster conception of the role of black men in the future of civilization." Disillusioned by massacres at home and blatant racism in many army camps abroad, Du Bois began to move further away from his white liberal and black militant supporters. "Fools," he said —"yes, that's it. Fools. All of us fools fought a long, cruel, bloody and unnecessary war and we not only killed our boys—

we killed Faith and Hope." Convinced now that colonialism and racial imperialism were the root causes of war, Du Bois began to see himself not only as a black leader but as a leader of all the colored peoples of the world. In 1919, he organized a pioneer Pan-African Congress in Paris. In the twenties, he held a series of Pan-African congresses — in London and Brussels in 1921, in London and Lisbon in 1923, in New York in 1927.

With the coming of the Great Depression, Du Bois re-evaluated his whole program and decided that the protest tradition he had spawned was doomed to futility. "By 1930," he said, "I had become convinced that the basic policies and ideals [of the NAACP] must be modified and changed; that in a world where economic dislocation has become so great as in ours, a mere appeal based on the old liberalism, a mere appeal to justice and further effort at legal decision, was missing the essential need; that the essential need was to guard and better the chances of Negroes, educated and ignorant, to earn a living, safeguard their income, and raise the level of their employment. I did not believe that a further prolongation of looking for salvation from the whites was feasible. So far as they were ignorant of the results of race prejudice, we had taught them; but so far as their race prejudice was built and increasingly built on the basis of the income which they enjoyed and their anti-Negro bias consciously or unconsciously formulated in order to protect their wealth and power, in so far our whole program must be changed, and we must seek to increase the power and particularly the economic organization among Negroes to meet the new situation...."

Du Bois was not then a Communist. Although he was impressed by the Russian "experiment," he had nothing but contempt for the American Communist party which was led, he said, "by a group of pitiable mental equipment, who gave no thought to the intricacies of the American situation, the vertical and horizontal divisions of the American working classes, and who plan simply to raise hell on any and all occasions, with Negroes as shock troops—these offer in reality nothing to us except social equality in jail." Du Bois was equally contemptous of the American labor movement, white liberalism, and the black elite. The only hope, he said, was "a magnificent crusade" based on a great leap by the black masses.

Beginning in January, 1934, Du Bois began to spell out the details of the crusade in the columns of the *Crisis*. Black people, he said, must use segregation to smash segregation. He called for the establishment of a "cooperative commonwealth" in the black ghetto, the organization of producer and consumer cooperatives, the socialization of the professional services of black doctors and lawyers, and a new ethic of leadership which would limit black leaders to small salaries. This program, which was in essence an anticipation of the Black Power movement, horrified NAACP leaders, who attacked Du Bois in the *Crisis* and were answered by Du Bois in the *Crisis*. The whole controversy became extremely heated, and Du Bois resigned in a huff and returned to Atlanta University.

Ideology apart, this was an act of extraordinary intellectual courage. For what Du Bois did now was to turn his back on twenty-five years of his life. He said that he now regarded the "income-bearing value of race prejudice" as "the cause not the result of prejudice" and "this conviction I had to express or spiritually die."

Although he was now sixty-six, Du Bois entered what was essentially his third career with a spurt of energy that would have distinguished a man half his age. During ten productive years at Atlanta University, he wrote two books, including the seminal *Black Reconstruction*, started work on an Afro-American encyclopedia, wrote a weekly newspaper column, founded *Phylon*, and lectured widely. He received a flood of tributes in these years, but he remained a disturbing and controversial figure. In 1944, his contract at Atlanta University was abruptly terminated and he returned to the NAACP with the vague title of director of special research. In this position, Du Bois gave special attention to colonial affairs. At the founding of the United Nations, he served as an associate counsel to the American delegation. After the San Francisco meeting, he revived the Pan-African movement, holding a very successful conference in London in October, 1945. This meeting, which was a milestone in the history of the colored peoples of the world, was attended by representatives from sixty nations and colonies, including Jomo Kenyatta and Kwame Nkrumah.

Throughout this period, Du Bois was the center of a series of internal disputes at NAACP headquarters. Two months before the 1948 election, in which he supported the Progressive party candidate, Du Bois was discharged from the NAACP with a pension.

There is no reason to think that Du Bois was right and his adversaries wrong in the interminable feuds that dotted his life. Du Bois was not an organization man. He was not an easy person to know or to work with. His presence in an organization, any organization, even his own organization, guaranteed internal strife. The old warrior said once that he loved a good fight, and he was not above going out of his way to pick one.

After leaving the NAACP, Du Bois abandoned the path of protest he had virtually invented and entered into an alliance with "progressive" and left-wing forces. In the next few years, he became an open advocate of "some form" of socialism, but he did not join the Communist party. "With my particular type of thinking and impulse," he said in 1948, "it was impossible for me to be a party man." Yet, he said openly that he would be a "fellow-traveler with Communist or capitalist, with white man or black" as long as "he walks towards the truth."

It seems that Du Bois maintained his independence in the left-wing camp. Biographer Francis L. Broderick noted that Du Bois "stubbornly rebuffed Communist efforts to induce him to testify at their trial" and turned thumbs down on other efforts to use him in ways not of his own choosing. Moreover, Du Bois' definition of socialism remained curiously unorthodox. He said on one occasion that the New Deal was just another name for socialism. Broderick concluded that Du Bois "appears to have remained master of his own thoughts — The Party did not set them for him. The alliance continued, at least until 1951, on Du Bois' own terms. On major issues — control of atomic energy, civil rights, the Korean War, the Marshall Plan — Du Bois sounded like an echo of the party's. Yet in all probability, Du Bois cooperated with Communists because on major issues they agreed with his independent views.... After all, Du Bois had been wary of white imperialism before the Russian Revolution of 1917; he had been thinking favorably about socialism at least as early as 1907; he had gone on record as a pacifist many times."

In 1949, Du Bois attended a series of international peace conferences. In 1950, he ran unsuccessfully as an American Labor party candidate in the New York senatorial race. That same year, 1950, he became chairman of the Peace Information Center, which was organized to agitate for peace and to secure American signatures on the "Stockholm Appeal," which demanded the absolute banning of atomic weapons. In 1951, Du Bois and four of his associates were indicted by a federal grand jury for failing to register the Peace Information Center as an alleged American agent of a foreign principal. Though Du Bois was acquitted at the trial, he was deeply affected by the whole episode and by the refusal of the government to permit him to travel to several events abroad (because of his failure to sign a non-Communist affidavit), including the Ghana independence celebration.

Out of pride perhaps or even perversity, Du Bois refused to modify his philosophy. In fact, as Broderick noted, he "deliberately" avoided "softening his line — no compromises, no equivocation," for, as Du Bois himself said: "I wanted to dispel in the minds of the government and of the public any lingering doubt as to my determination to think and speak freely on the economic foundations of the wars and the frustrations of the twentieth century."

To the end, Du Bois maintained a keen interest in the Freedom movement. He was particularly encouraged by the audacity of the black youth who initiated the sit-in age in 1960. Asked if he had any advice for the sit-in students, Du Bois said: "They don't need any advice from me. Perhaps I need some from them."

After the Supreme Court invalidated the non-Communist affidavit provision, Du Bois left America and wandered across the face of the world. "In my own country," he said, "for nearly half a century I have been nothing but a nigger." Old, weary, ninety-three years of age, he entered the Communist party.

On the invitation of President Nkrumah, who considered him "the father of Pan-Africanism," Du Bois moved to Accra, Ghana. With his second wife, author Shirley Graham, whom he married in 1951 after the death of his first wife, Du Bois settled down in a comfortable cottage and began work on an *Encyclopedia Africana.* There, at the end of the trail, on the eve of the mammoth March on Washington, W. E. B. Du Bois died at 10:40, Tuesday night, August 27, 1963. The next day, the *Ghanaian Times* printed a bold black headline.

THIS DAY A MIGHTY TREE HAS FALLEN IN AFRICA

A long way from the white snow of Great Barrington, a long way from the peach trees of Atlanta, in a new land he called home, Du Bois was laid to rest in a plot of ground where the surf meets the sea that carried his forefathers to America decades ago. It was a gesture that would have pleased the poet. The wheel had come full cycle—from Africa to Africa, from freedom to Freedom.

Large in life, even larger in death, Du Bois received memorial

tributes from left-wingers and right-wingers, liberals and con-
servatives, Tories and radicals. In a radio tribute, President
Kwame Nkrumah of Ghana said: "The essential quality of Dr.
Du Bois' life and achievement can be summed up in a single
phrase—intellectual honesty and integrity." Thirty prominent
Americans (James Baldwin, John Hope Franklin, John Haynes
Holmes, Roy Wilkins and others) who sponsored a memorial
tribute to Du Bois in Carnegie Hall perceived similar qualities
in the old fighter's life. The aim of the memorial tribute, as
stated by actor and playwright Ossie Davis, was "to secure to
the Afro-American consciousness the personality, image, and
cultural significance of the most illustrious Afro-American
scholar of our time, and to present to Americans at large a
proper sense of Dr. Du Bois' intellectual contribution to
American life."

Even in death, Du Bois characteristically had the last word.
Feeling death coming, he had written, six years before, his last
message to the world. The message was read at his funeral.

*It is much more difficult in theory than actually to say the last
goodbye to one's loved ones and friends and to all the familiar things
of this life.*

*I am going to take a long, deep and endless sleep. This is not a
punishment but a privilege to which I have looked forward for years.*

*I have loved my work. I have loved people and my play but always
I have been uplifted by the thought that what I have done well will live
long and justify my life: that what I have done ill or never finished
can now be handed on to others for endless days to be finished, perhaps
better than I could have done. And that peace will be my applause.*

*One thing alone I charge you as you live and believe in life. Always
human beings will live and progress to greater, broader and fuller
life. The only possible death is to lose belief in this truth simply because
the great end comes slowly; because time is long.*

Goodbye.

INDEX

Index

Index

Index